Coming of Age

Published by
Kachere Series
P.O. Box 1037, Zomba, Malawi
ISBN: 99908-76-52-5 (Kachere Texts no. 25)
ISBN-13: 978-99908-76-52-9

The Kachere Series is represented outside Africa by
African Books Collective, Oxford (orders@africanbookscollective.com)
Michigan State University Press, East Lansing, MI (msupress@msu.edu)

Layout and cover design: Mercy Chilunga

Printed by Lightning Source

Coming of Age

A Christianized Initiation for Women in Southern Malawi

Rachel Nyagondwe Fiedler

Kachere Texts no. 25

Kachere Series
Zomba
2005

Kachere Series
P.O. Box 1037, Zomba, Malawi
kachere@globemw.net
www.sdnp.org.mw/kachereseries/

This book is part of the Kachere Series, a range of books on religion, culture and society from Malawi. Other Kachere titles are:

Rachel Nyagondwe Banda, *Women of Bible and Culture: Baptist Convention Women in Southern Malawi.*

J.W.M. van Breugel, *Chewa Traditional Religion.*

Maria Saur, Linda Semu and Stella Hauya Ndau, *Nkhanza: Listening to People's Voices.*

David Mphande, *Nthanthi za Chitonga za Kusambizgiya ndi Kutauliya.*

Joseph C. Chakanza (ed.) *Research in African Traditional Religion: Initiation Rites for Boys in Lomwe Society and other Essays.*

Andy G. Khumbanyiwa, *Kufa ndi Ludzu Mwendo Uli M'madzi.*

Joseph C. Chakanza (ed.), *Utumiki wa Amai Mumpingo M'bindikiro wa Amai.*

Mulungu wa Chikondi ndi wa Chifundo: Malingaliro a Chikhristu pa Edzi.

White et. al, *Dispossessing the Widow: Gender Based Violence in Malawi.*

Janet Y. Kholowa ndi Klaus Fiedler, *Pachiyambi Anawalenga Chimodzimodzi.*

WLSA, *In Search of Justice: Women and the Administration of Justice in Malawi.*

Isabel Apawo Phiri, *Women, Presbyterianism and Patriarchy: Religious Experience of Chewa Women in Central Malawi.*

Treasuring the Gift: How to Handle God's Gift of Sex

The Kachere Series is the publications arm of the Department of Theology and Religious Studies of the University of Malawi.

Series Editors: J.C. Chakanza, Fulata L. Moyo, F.L. Chingota. Klaus Fiedler, P.A. Kalilombe, Martin Ott, Shareef Mohammad

FOREWORD

There is something mysterious in growing up. And it is a long and sometimes cumbersome process. When Lovenesi and Maga play family they
may not imagine how long it will take them to be mother and father in
real life. If it is not easy for children to grow up, it is not easy for their
parents either. These little ones were so nice and then suddenly they
turn 13 (I am not assuming that trouble necessarily starts at 13, nor do I
assume that there is no trouble before that age, but memories often
make it look like that.) And if the children and their parents are concerned about growing up and how life is to be transmitted to the next
generation, then society as a whole should be concerned on how to
manage that process of growing up with its troubles and mysteries.

Virtually all African societies have constructed very specific initiation
rites around that process of growing up. In some societies such rites
were very extensive like among the Chagga, where the teachings given
at the various stages, with their German translation, fill over 3000
pages[1], and that is for boys only. Other African societies may have less
elaborate coming of age rituals, but they all show a responsibility to
guide the young people from childhood to a childhood, not denying the
responsibility of mother and father, aunts (especially the maternal ones)
and uncles (from both sides).

While the elaborate transition rites of the Chagga do not take place
any longer, initiation is still an important feature of almost all African societies, even among the Chagga and many other societies that have
shortened the process.

The very first missionaries who came to these parts of Africa took little
note of initiation, since it was not yet an issue.[2] But when initiation came
to be noticed as an issue the church had to deal with, the reaction of the
missionaries varied greatly, from outright rejection via uneasy toleration

---

[1]   The last of the great teaching elders transmitted the accumulated teachings together with his staff of authority, to Bruno Guttmann, the missionary of Moshi-
Mbokomu at that time.
[2]   The first missionaries came to [Old] Moshi in 1885, the issue of girls' circumcision
was brought up for the first time in the elders' council in 1910.

to full scale Christianization. So it came to pass that in Kenya around 1930 the missionaries of the Africa Inland Mission and of the Presbyterian Mission vehemently opposed girls' circumcision, that the Catholics saw no problems in it and made no riot, while the Anglicans chose the local option, leaving it to the station missionaries to decide to join the fight or to keep out of it.

As the missionaries differed in their attitudes, so differed the African Christians in theirs. While among the Kikuyu Christians there was only a small minority who demanded a ban on girls' circumcision, among the Lutheran Christians on the slopes of Mt Kilimanjaro in neighbouring Tanzania, circumcision was abolished in 1924 by the African leaders of the church, with no missionary being involved, since they had almost all been repatriated to Germany due to the Versailles Peace Treaty.

And to make matters a little more complicated, when the German missionaries came back in 1926, they made sure that the laws forbidding circumcision were immediately rescinded. Quite paternalistic how they behaved, but most Lutheran Christians were delighted.

Closer to Malawi, it was the Anglican Bishop of Masasi, Vincent Lucas, who, after being requested by the Yao Christians there, organized a full Christianization of the Yao transition rites, starting with the boys'. The Masasi Christians retained the camp in the bush, and to it the *ngariba* would come with his sharp knife and extra long thumb nail like to the camps of old, but the teaching would be Christian, and since after the [traditional] operation the [modern] dresser from the hospital would come to dress the wounds, they would heal much faster, and in a short time the Christian boys' circumcision had all but driven out the traditional one.

When trying to apply the same principle to the girls' transition rite, Bishop Lucas faltered at first and decreed that in all girls' camps a white missionary lady had to be present. The effect was that even some of the mature Christian church women would put their daughters through the Christian girls' rite first and then through the traditional one, to get the real thing. It took Lucas some time and some advice to take the missionary lady out of the equation, leave the decision, what to teach and how to dramatize it, to the women elders in the camp and their Christian consciences.

Bishop Lucas' policies had some influence in Malawi. Though the Anglicans here belonged to a different diocese, the two dioceses of Masasi and Lake Malawi belong both to the same mission, Universities Mission to Central Africa. In the Catholic Church various attempts were made to come to terms with the issue of initiation, which were not an unmitigated success. Blantyre Synod struggled in a similar way. Much more success-ful was Nkhoma Synod, which - in the 1940s turned the traditional *chinamwali* into the Christian *chilangizo*, a rite that was accepted, despite its deep differences to the traditional rite, on equal terms with it.

The Baptist Convention came to Malawi only in 1960, but having one of its centres around Lilongwe among the matrilineal Chewa and another around Jali among the mixed but equally matrilineal population there, did not fail to address the issue of girls' initiation. In a cooperation between local and missionary women, a booklet was compiled for the *alangizi* in charge of the initiation of Baptist girls. This led to a reduction of the rite from 3 days and nights to one hour or less, and all the fun and excite-ment (and most of the mystery) was taken out as well.[3] While the booklet was obviously applied with some success in the Central Region,[4] in the Southern Region it was only applied once, and only for one girl, and then quietly laid aside. Here in the South in some Baptist Convention congre-gations the girls attend the traditional (*bwalo*) *chinamwali*, but other con-gregations have organized their own Christian *chinamwali*, without a writ-ten base, but lasting three days and nights, and being full of singing, dancing, drama and excitement—and probably some frustration, too. While it keeps the traditional frame, it has a clear Christian intention. Its strength is that is was developed and is being sustained without impetus from either the missionaries or the Baptist Convention office. To use a current slogan, it is a grassroots initiation.

This initiation, as all the others, has its own rules. Initiation rites are transition rites, which take a person from a lower level in society to a higher level. But between the two is the "camp", the liminal phase, in which the initiates are taken away from society, are secluded, to be initi-ated into the mysteries of life. This liminal phase is not only characterized by physical distance and by restricted attendance, but also by different language rules. What is otherwise taboo, like sexuality, can and must be

---

[3] Often aggravated by the fact that the lady who reads the text (a reading lasts about 15 minutes) is not a good reader, and most likely she will read the instructions to the teacher and the information for the girl in a row without even modulating the tone of her voice.

[4] Though one may doubt if taking all the excitement out of the rite is a success.

spoken about freely—though not without reverence, since all the mystery of life is involved.

Sexuality, one of God's great gifts to humankind, has always been in danger of abuse, and initiation rites are one way to help protect that gift from being abused. Since the 1980s, the blessings of sexuality have been further endangered by HIV/Aids, which can make marriage—one of God's original blessings—a death trap. Initiation, traditional as its forms are, is one possibility to strengthen girls against these new dangers, and as readers you are invited to see how such a rite, Christian and traditional at the same time, has taken up the challenge.

The rite described in this book was produced not by scholars, theologians or consultants, but in real life, by churches and mothers. Teaching, quite appropriately, is often conveyed by songs, which remain in memory better than the words of a teacher, since the songs are repeated at every *chinamwali* a woman, once initiated, attends. Here, for the first time to my knowledge—at least for this region of Africa—there is a full record of all the teaching songs, of the context in which they were presented, and of the drama produced in connection with some of them. In addition, though the record is not verbatim, much of the verbal teaching associated with the songs is also given.

Initiation is about the mysteries of life—and therefore precious. It is endangered, too. There is the danger—often seen by the churches—that initiation may not promote the moral life. There is the danger that good Christian intentions to purify the initiation process may reduce it to a ritual that does not help the girls in any way in their quest to grow up and be women. There is also the danger, that girls may be denied any initiation because it is too costly, or comes at the wrong time for the family. And there is also the danger of modernity, where speed is of the essence. Everywhere in Africa initiation rituals are being shortened, and if they are shortened too much, they may be reduced to nothing in the end or to a ritual with neither instruction nor learning.

In order to help safeguard a valuable tool for society in the transmission of the mysteries of life to the next generation, this book is being published. Girls initiation is still much sought after, it has much potential to help improve and safeguard life, and with this in mind, it may need improvement and further development. For this reason the author offers the record of one *chinamwali* to the public, asking her readers to treat the texts—and the mysteries therein—with the respect they deserve.

Her thanks go to the church somewhere here in the south, that made her, a Tumbuka, welcome to attend the initiation in a different cultural setting, to write down the songs—and to be initiated herself. That no names are mentioned is due to the character of the material presented, but her thanks are heartily offered to all who helped her in what was originally part of her research for a University degree, but can hopefully be of wider usefulness.

May I—once her postgraduate supervisor—add my good wishes for the publication of this book. May it help to promote and protect life, God's great gift.

Klaus Fiedler
Zomba, Lent 2005

CHRISTIANIZED *CHINAMWALI* FOR WOMEN IN BAPTIST CHURCHES IN SOUTHERN MALAWI

In general, the majority of indigenous Africans struggle to protect their heritage of initiation rites against outside influences such as westernization, urbanization and/or Christianization. With this in mind even the Church seeks ways of preserving them without tarnishing the gospel, and this is being done in an exercise known as inculturation or contextualization as others prefer. This exercise involves debates ranging from either rejecting them completely to conserving them all. These extremes are easier to achieve although they are unlikely to be popular among the majority of the grassroots Christians who have initiation at the centre of their culture. The midfield is the most interesting one and crucial in the exercise of inculturation. It seeks to retain the positive elements and remove or adapt the negative elements in the initiation ceremonies with a view of avoiding syncretism or oppression to the participants.

Available literature

Scholars, both native and non-native, have written concerning initiation of girls and boys in Africa, because of its impact on the initiates as well as the society and the church. In these writings, one of the common threads has been the attitude both the locals and non-locals have towards it.[1] However the church is concerned about the inculturation of these rites. As such there have been many works on Christianization of

---

[1] J.C. Chakanza for example writes on the attitude of the Roman Catholic Church in Southern Malawi towards puberty rites of boys and girls for a period of 70 years. See J.C. Chakanza, "The Unfinished Agenda: Puberty Rites and the Response of the Roman Catholic Church in Southern Malawi, 1901-1994", *Religion in Malawi* 5, 1995, p. 3.

initiation rites especially in Roman Catholic[2] as well as other church traditions such as Nkhoma Synod,[3] Blantyre Synod,[4] Providence Industrial
Mission[5] and the Anglican Church.[6] On the women's side, the crucial issue is how initiation is liberating to the girl child. As such their writings
are aimed at creating awareness of the shortfalls in initiation and also of
the positive aspects in it, which must be defended. It is to this that this
Christianized initiation of girls and women in the Baptist Church makes a
contribution.

A few female scholars have written about African traditional rites. Isabel Phiri has discussed the issue as regards the Presbyterian women of
Nkhoma Synod.[7] She writes on the roles of traditional initiation for
women in the society and the attitude of missionaries that led to its ban
and to the introduction of *chilangizo* (Christian initiation) and the success
and deficiencies of it.[8]

Elvira Ignasio has described the activities, lessons and methods util-
ized in both the traditional and Christianized pre-puberty and puberty
rites among Yao girls in Nankhwali area [9] Her contribution is how the
Catholic Church has responded to the traditional pre-puberty and puberty

---

[2]   Such as Elvira M. Ignasio, The Christianization of the Traditional Pre-puberty and
Puberty Rites for Girls and its Effects on the Society around Nankhwali Area, Monkey-Bay, BA, University of Malawi, 1998; J.C. Chakanza. "The Unfinished Agenda:
Puberty Rites and the Response of the Roman Catholic Church in Southern Malawi,
1901-1994, *Religion in Malawi* 5, 1995, p. 3.
[3]   Isabel Apawo Phiri, *Women, Presbyterianism and Patriarchy. Religious Experiences of Chewa Women in Central Malawi.* Blantyre: CLAIM-Kachere, 2000, pp. 38,
62-79.
[4]   Felix Chingota, "A Historical Account of the Attitude of Blantyre Synod of the
Church of Central Africa Presbyterian towards Initiation Rites", *Religion in Malawi*
1995, pp. 8-13.
[5]   Patrick Makondesa, "Christian Initiation Rites in Southern Malawi" MA Module 1,
Department of Theology and Religious Studies, University of Malawi, 1999.
[6]   Martin Mgeni, "Girls' initiation in a Yao Setting and Christian Attitude: Case Study
at Msembuka Village – Chikala Plateau – T/A Chamba, Msondo Rite". Class presentation, Department of TRS, University of Malawi, 1996.
[7]   Isabel Phiri, *Women, Presbyterianism and Patriarchy,* p. 38, pp. 62-79.
[8]   Ibid, p. 62. See also Isabel Apawo Phiri, "Christianity: Liberative or Oppressive to
African Women" in Kenneth R. Ross (ed.), *Faith at the Frontiers of Knowledge,* Blantyre: CLAIM-Kachere, 1998, pp. 198-217.
[9]   Elvira M. Ignasio, The Christianization of the Traditional Pre-Puberty and Puberty
Rites for Girls and its Effects on the Society around Nankhwali Area, Monkey-Bay,
BA, University of Malawi, 1998.

rites, as well as success and deficiencies in this process. While she shows the possible reason for the negative perceptions concerning the traditional rites missionaries had, my concern is how Baptist women, at present, perceive traditional initiation and church initiation. Additionally, even though Elvira Ignasio concludes with a central argument which is also my interest, that there are liberating as well as oppressive elements in girls' initiation she does not give a comprehensive analysis of this truth. I want to expand on this as regards lessons, methods and activities involved in one complete Christianized initiation. However, since I have not participated in a traditional initiation, Elvira's work is a valuable contribution to the knowledge of traditional initiation, for purposes of comparison to the Christianized initiation, although it is written about girls of a different area and faith.

Although the issue of initiation is crucial to women, it is mostly men who have written concerning this. Orison Chaponda has written about Christianized Yao rites of Mangochi Catholic Diocese.[10] Orison Chaponda gives a local example of some of the missionaries' attempt to Christianize Yao rites. In this he agrees with Klaus Fiedler, that not all missionaries were negative to traditional rites.[11] His research is a contribution in showing what factors have contributed to the rejection and acceptance of this Christianized rite within the Catholic Church of Mangochi Diocese. In this he provides points of comparison as to what are the likely dangers to developing a Christianized initiation as this can be applied to the Baptist Church.

Martin Mgeni has also written about girls' initiation among the Yao at Msembuka Village.[12] He gives a description of the procedure in the

---

[10]   Orison Chaponda, "The Christianized Yao Initiation rite of Mangochi Catholic Diocese: Assessing an Experiment in Inculturation", MA module 2, 1979, University of Malawi.
[11]   See Klaus Fiedler, "Christianity and African Culture. Conservative German Protestant Missionaries in Tanzania, 1900-1940", Blantyre: CLAIM-Kachere, 1999. Also Klaus Fiedler, "Bishop Lucas' Christianization of Traditional Rites, the Kikuyu Female Circumcision Controversy and the 'Cultural Approach' of Conservative German Missionaries in Tanzania", in Robin Lamburn, *From a Missionary's Notebook*. The Yao of Tunduru and other Essays, Saarbrücken, 1991.
[12]   Martin Mgeni, "Girls Initiation in a Yao Setting and Christian Attitude, Case Study at Msembuka Village – Chikala Plateau, T.A. Chamba, Nsondo Rite," Class Presentation, Department of TRS, University of Malawi, 1996.

nsondo rite,[13] which until 1959 involved the removal of the *labia minora* by a sharp instrument. This was later replaced by drinking an herbal medicine that is believed to reduce the *labia minora*. His contribution is to give a variety of another kind of initiation rite girls go through, and the effect it has on the girls and the society. He also briefly shows how the Anglican Church has inculturated this rite. However his seven line account on the subject is very brief,[14] but forms another background of how effective inculturation of traditional rites is in other church traditions and how they compare and contrast with the Christianized initiation done by Baptist women in the south.

Orison Chaponda also writes on the initiation of boys and men in the Chewa culture, that of *gule wamkulu*.[15] Although this subject is not on girls' initiation, his research is an important contribution to stages and challenges of inculturation, which is a central issue in the Christianization of girls' initiation. It therefore contributes to an understanding of the development of Christianized initiation among Baptist women. Nevertheless, there has been no systematic study of the Christianized initiation for women in the Baptist Church.[16]

The situation: Forms of initiation rites and perceptions

There are variations in the Christianization of initiation rites in the Baptist Convention churches in the Southern region. This is because of a wide selection of cultural groupings in this area. In some places, the *Buku la Alangizi* has been adopted, and where this is done, it is referred to as

---

[13]   Girls' rites have different names depending on type and cultural group. *Nsondo* rite for example is *chiputu* rite among the Amang'anja. The instructors also are given different names depending on cultural groupings, for example *anakanga* among the Yao and *anankungwi* among the Chewa, the initiates also have different names depending on cultural groupings such as *wali* or *namwali*.
[14]   See Martin Mgeni, Girls' Initiation in a Yao Setting and Christian Attitude, p. 2.
[15]   Orison J.T. Chaponda, *Gule Wamkulu* in the Catholic Church, Lilongwe Rural. A Cultural Phenomenon and a Pastoral Problem. M.A. Module, University of Malawi.
[16]   Molly Longwe was the first one to make an extensive study of initiation among the Chewa Baptist women of Lilongwe district for her MTh in African Christianity: Molly Longwe, From *Chinamwali* to *Chilangizo*: the Christianization of Pre-Christian Chewa Initiation Rites in the Baptist Convention of Malawi, MTh, University of Natal, 2003.

chilangizo.[17] However the traditional initiation for girls is also diverse in Southern Malawi.

South South region

In this region, the traditional initiation ceremonies are not called *chinamwali*, they are referred to as *dzoma*. In the Lower Shire, among the *Lomwe*, only one type of *dzoma* is done – *dzoma lalikulu* (initiation after puberty). Among the Mang'anja of Lower Shire and Thyolo, they have *dzoma laling'ono* (initiation before puberty) as well.[18] The initiates are called *buthu*. Therefore this initiation before puberty is also called *chibuthu*.

Baptist women in the Lower Shire and Thyolo are not always free to send girls to *dzoma laling'ono*. Those who do this, can loose membership if discovered.[19] In Mpando Baptist Church a member joined the church before puberty. The mother sent her to *dzoma laling'ono* and the church disciplined the girl. She left the Baptist church and joined the Apostolic Faith Church.[20] The church's alternative to traditional initiation ceremonies in the South South region is *chilangizo*.[21]

Perception against dzoma

The church has no problem with *dzoma lalikulu* but with *dzoma laling'ono*. The reasons given are relating to age and content. *Dzoma laling'ono* is not good because girls are taught things that are beyond their age. As such the initiation ceremony is perceived to defile the girls (*kulaula*). The songs at *dzoma* are considered as profane, as such, the church discourages parents to send their girls to these initiation ceremonies.

One example of songs that the church sees as an example of profane songs is as follows:

---

[17] *Buku la Alangizi*, Baptist Convention of Malawi, Lilongwe: Baptist Publications, nd.
[18] Int. focus group, Nsomo Baptist Church and focus group, Mpando Baptist Church, Thyolo, 26.7.2000.
[19] Int. Mrs Mary Mafuule, Mpando Baptist Church, Thyolo, 26.7.2000.
[20] Ibid.
[21] *Chilangizo* is also a name of Christianized initiation ceremonies in Nkhoma Synod among Chewa women. See Isabel Phiri, *Women, Presbyterianism and Patriarchy*, p. 108.

Machende, mbolo phwi,	Testicles, penis together,
Mbolongunda,	Penis,
Eee, ee.	Eeeh, eeh.

Such a song is considered inappropriate for Christian girl children. However, the church accepts *dzoma lalikulu*.[22] And this is what is adapted to
the Christianized initiation and then called *chilangizo*.

Chilangizo

In the South South region, they have two types of *chilangizo*: *Chilangizo
cha ana*, and *chilangizo* for those getting married. *Chilangizo cha ana* is
also called *ulangizo wa atsikana*, and it is the initiation for girls after puberty. The positive perceptions as regards this church initiation are
based on the following: the initiates are at a good age between 15 and
18 years, *chilangizo* lasts only two to three days, as opposed to one
week in the traditional initiation, *chilangizo* excludes unnecessary things
such as profane language and concentrates on real issues that affect
girls that have reached puberty such as instructing the girl on how to
dress up and on cleanliness during menstruation.

The second *chilangizo* is for girls who are nearly getting married. This
chilangizo before marriage revolves around submission of the wife in the
family, general cleanliness and industriousness. However, some of the
things done before marriage in certain congregations can be shocking.[23]
Among the Sena, after *chilangizo* the bride and bridegroom are requested to have sex before their day of wedding. This is done to check
whether the woman is a virgin, and also to check whether the man will be
able to have children. This ceremony is usually undertaken under the
guidance of the *ankhoswe* of the bride and of the bridegroom and a
member of the church. The future couple is given a piece of cloth and
asked to have sexual intercourse in one of the rooms while the *ankhoswe* and the member of the church wait in the other room. After sex,
they would use the cloth to wipe off the sperms and surrender the cloth
to them. By studying the piece of cloth, they are able to tell whether the
girl was a virgin or not. If she was, there will be traces of blood. They

---

[22] Int. Mrs Mary Mafuule, Mpando Baptist Church, 26.7.2000.
[23] Int. member x, Soche Baptist Church, 1999.

also detect whether the man will have children if the cloth sticks together when dry.[24]

South East region

Baptist women in the South East enjoy relative freedoms in their participation in *chinamwali*. There are two types of *chinamwali* that Baptist women engage in, in this region: church *chinamwali* and *bwalo chinamwali* (*chinamwali cha chikunja* - traditional initiation). Both of these are actively supported by Baptist women, and Baptist women engage themselves in them freely without fear of getting disciplined by their church as is the case with other churches such as the CCAP of Blantyre Synod[25] and the Roman Catholic Church[26] as well as in some Baptist Churches in the South South region.[27] Baptist women in the South East go through four major categories of initiation: *chinamwali cha ana* (for small girls), *chiputu* (for those girls who have reached puberty), *litiwo* (for those with first pregnancy or child), and *kuweramira ana* (bowing for children) for those with grandchildren. These were also observed during the church *chinamwali* in the South East demonstrating that these major categories in the traditional initiation are just as important in the church *chinamwali*.

In a survey of Baptist churches in the South East region *bwalo chinamwali* is more widely supported than church *chinamwali*. In a sample of twenty three girls, in the wider Zomba area, only six girls had attended church *chinamwali* and seventeen of them attended *bwalo chinamwali*. All the six girls that were initiated through church *chinamwali* also at-

---

[24] Sena women, *Ulangizi* Seminar, South East region, Zomba Baptist Church, 3.8.2000. Such things are also done in other cultures such as the Yao of Likoma. They are taught at the *nsondo* rite that white sticky sperms signify fertility. See Renata Sakaike, Collection of Materials. Nsondo Rites, 1996, p. 2.
[25] See Felix Chingota, "A Historical Account of the Attitude of Blantyre Synod of the Church of Central Africa Presbyterian towards Initiation Rites", *Religion in Malawi* No 5, 1995, p. 12. Chingota points out that parents are disciplined if they send their girl children to the traditional initiation.
[26] See J.C. Chakanza "The Unfinished Agenda: Puberty Rites and the Response of the Roman Catholic Church in Southern Malawi, 1901-1994, *Religion in Malawi* No 5, 1995, pp. 3-7, for example p. 6. Parents are banned from participation in the sacraments and have to attend instructions before confession.
[27] In Nkhoma Synod, the church gives a penalty of eighteen months suspension from sacraments for the parents. Isabel Apawo Phiri, *Women, Presbyterianism and Patriarchy*, p. 69.

tended *bwalo chinamwali*. Similarly, all the seventeen that were initiated through *bwalo chinamwali* also attended a church *chinamwali*.[28]

Nevertheless, when all the girls were asked as to which type of *chinamwali* they would prefer, all were in support of church *chinamwali* and some argued that they were initiated through *bwalo chinamwali* because their congregations did not hold church *chinamwali* or they were forced by their sponsors who were usually parents or relatives. Since *chinamwali* is very important to them, they argued that they had no option, but to go to *bwalo chinamwali*.[29] However, the fact that girls initiated through church *chinamwali* also participated in *bwalo chinamwali*, show that their preference of church *chinamwali* over *bwalo chinamwali* is not because *bwalo chinamwali* is bad, but for other reasons.

Not all churches in the South East region hold church *chinamwali*. In these churches, the majority of girls go for *bwalo chinamwali*. This was the case with the seventeen girls who went for *bwalo chinamwali*. Their churches did not hold church *chinamwali*. Some of the girls that claim to have observed church *chinamwali* observed those organized by other churches such as Blantyre Synod and PIM.[30] However, there are also girls in Baptist churches who do not go to any *chinamwali*. In addition to the twenty-three girls that were interviewed, two girls were deliberately removed from the sample because they did not go through any initiation due to illnesses in their family. The reasons why some girls are not initiated are economic, theological as well as cultural. Economic, because these initiation ceremonies are expensive and sickness in a family may even increase that expense. But others perceive *chinamwali* as satanic and unsuitable for a genuine believer in Christ.[31]

Nevertheless, both church and society accept church *chinamwali* as well as *bwalo chinamwali* although with a few reservations, which do not disadvantage girls from being fully accepted members of church and society.[32] This is probably because this church *chinamwali* has adopted the

---

[28] Int. girls at Youth South East Region conference, Zomba Baptist Church, 23.12.2000.
[29] Ibid.
[30] Ibid.
[31] This opinion was the minority in each focus group.
[32] Others perceive church *chinamwali* as lacking important details such as dancing while naked.

method of teaching in the traditional initiation and has retained most of its teachings.

The girls in the sample came from a diverse cultural background. Fourteen came from families where the mother was Nyanja married to a Yao; three girls had Yao mothers and Nyanja fathers; three girls had both parents who were Nyanja, two girls had parents where the mother was Tumbuka and the father was Yao and one girl had parents who were both Chewa. The diversity of mixed marriages portrays that Baptist women are exposed to a wide range of types of initiation.[33] This diversity is also a challenge to the *ulangizi* seminars these women participate in. *Ulangizi* seminars, therefore, have to be designed so that they benefit women from such diverse backgrounds.[34] As such reference to one type of initiation, such as Yao initiation, during discussions would not be sufficient for Baptist women in this area. They therefore look for a mechanism that will bring in elements from various types of initiation. From these findings, it is also seen that Baptist women are not restricted to marrying men of their own tribes. Their choices in marriage are shaped by their tastes,[35] unless they have been forced to marry by parents. In an interview with the twenty-three girls above, some of the girls expressed that some are forced to marry for economic reasons. Some of the economic reasons given were that parents desire to see their girls marry before they die so that they would have someone to depend on. Secondly it may be that the man the girl is forced to marry has a paid job in town to benefit the girl as well as her parents. Those girls, who go against their parents' wishes, are sometimes punished by denying them their rights such as school fees and food.[36] According to these girls, forced marriages are another contributing factor to the increased divorce rate and HIV endemic in the region. This is because they marry men whose moral backgrounds are not known. The latter is conducive to HIV, especially since HIV tests before marriage are very rare in Malawi.

---

[33] See appendix song no. 8 suggesting three major types of initiation: *Wachilomwe, wa Jando,* and wa *Chidototo.*

[34] For details on *Ulangizi* Seminars see Rachel Nyagondwe Banda, *Women of Bible and Culture: Baptist Convention Women in Southern Malawi,* Zomba: Kachere, 2005, pp 184-186.

[35] See appendix song no. 8 suggesting women desiring men with different forms of initiation.

[36] Int. z, x, girls at Youth South East regional conference, Zomba Baptist Church, 23.12.2000.

Perceptions on bwalo chinamwali[37]

The following reasons were given against women participating in *bwalo chinamwali*: obscene language, sexually suggestive movements in the dance and language in the songs,[38] sexual demonstrations, a young child is told everything that parents do in marriage and this makes them to be rude to their elders people, they do not do proper things at the ceremonies and it is not for children of born again parents. Hence, the reasons given are related to age, theology, content and method.

The following reasons were given by those in support of chinamwali: Baptist pastors who are chiefs also hold this *chinamwali* in their village; Baptist women are not only Christians but also ATR believers; it is the right of a girl child to go through the traditionally accepted *chinamwali* that the parents went through; in the absence of church *chinamwali*, children have no option but to go to *bwalo chinamwali*; in church *chinamwali*, where will the *alangizi* get the traditional medicine to protect the initiates; there is no teaching on the shortfalls in the traditional *chinamwali*; church *chinamwali* is not orderly (*siwolongosoka*); to avoid their girls to be despised by friends who have gone through traditional *chinamwali* as *wodyera ku nkhonkho* (those who eat with their elbow); and there is disorganization at regional and associational level as regards the role of instituted *alangizi* in the Baptist Church. As such they do not do their job and instead, *bwalo chinamwali* is opted for.

Those that are against *bwalo chinamwali* do not necessarily send their girls to a church *chinamwali*, because of various reasons. They argue that it is syncretistic, for example, although a prayer is offered at the beginning and at the end, the rest in the ceremony is done as in *bwalo chinamwali*.[39] Others believe that those who are born again cannot send their children even for church initiation. Some of these believe that individual counselling of girls is sufficient.[40] However, church *chinamwali* is well supported in churches that hold them.

---

[37] Both negative and positive perceptions are not only distinct to Baptists but other church groups as well. For such perceptions among Catholics, see J.C. Chakanza, "The Unfinished Agenda. Puberty Rites and the Response of the Roman Catholic Church in Southern Malawi, 1940-1994", *Religion in Malawi* No 5, 1995, p. 5.
[38] Int. Member, Soche Baptist Church.
[39] Int. focus group, Mwanafumu Baptist Church, Jali, 21.3.2000.
[40] At Makolije Baptist Church, Mrs Kanichi does individual counselling. Int. focus group, Makolije Baptist Church. 22.3.2000.

There are others who do not send children to either *bwalo chinamwali* or Christian initiation because they cannot afford the costs of sending their girls there. Nevertheless it should be noted that girls have little choice to choose what kind of initiation they want. Choices are mostly made by their sponsors.

Comparison between Christianized and traditional initiation

From the perceptions above, it is clear that church initiation and traditional initiation among Baptists have similarities and differences. The similarities are shown in the fact that certain elements are shared by both, though not all. However it is such differences and similarities that are the foundation for the inculturation exercise.

In the South South the similarity is that both *chilangizo* and *dzoma* have two ceremonies. In *chilangizo*, there is the initiation of girls after reaching puberty and then for those who are about to get married. In *dzoma* there is initiation for the girls before puberty (*dzoma laling'ono*) and for those after puberty (*dzoma lalikulu*). Although in both cases there are two ceremonies, the only similarity is that *chilangizo* for girls is based on *dzoma lalikulu*. However, there is no equivalent of *dzoma laling'ono* in the *chilangizo*.

In the traditional setup, *dzoma lalikulu* is aimed at preparing girls for marriage, as such, there is no traditional initiation targeted for marriage alone. The other difference is that traditional initiation begins with young girls from around five years old whereas in *chilangizo*, it is only girls that have reached puberty who go through the initiation. Also *chilangizo* takes a much shorter time than traditional initiation. The other difference is that *chilangizo* is held in a church building, while the traditional initiation is held in a house, usually at the chief's homestead.

In the South East the differences and similarities between church *chinamwali* and *bwalo chinamwali* can be assessed when an analysis of one Christianized initiation in this region is done. The documentation of one complete church *chinamwali* in this book is the basis of this analysis. However it should be noted that there can never be only one type of Christianized initiation in this region because cultures differ. Since in this region cultures have fused over the years,[41] it is difficult having a pure

---

[41] In the area of my research, the main cultures are Yao, Nyanja, Mang'anja, Lomwe and Chewa.

tribal initiation ceremony. Other than comparing the traditional and the Christianized initiation, the central aim of this analysis focuses on investigating whether this particular Christianized initiation is liberating or oppressing to the women in the Baptist Convention. This assessment does not claim to be exhaustive but it gives an adequate representative picture of church *chinamwali* in some congregations in the South East in particular.[42]

Teaching in Baptist *chinamwali*

In this *chinamwali*, the teaching can be grouped in several major areas. In each area, there will be discussions whether the teachings are liberating and/or oppressing to the girls or the women, as well as suggestions of improvements in methods and content. The following major areas of content such as teaching on sex, taking initiation seriously, general good behaviour, African traditional religion and general marriage issues (with their methods such as drama, songs and figurative language) will be treated.

To take the initiation seriously

This teaching is presented largely through songs, although societal pressure not to consider one as an adult in society is also a great push for girls to go for initiation. When a girl has not gone through initiation she is considered to be too young to participate in activities such as funerals and watching an initiation dance itself. Lack of initiation therefore denies girls a certain status in society and in turn oppresses the girls. The girl without initiation does not only suffer alienation from the society but is also perceived to be incompetent to run a marriage because initiation is conceived to be the only way a girl gets educated on matters relating to marriage. The possibility that a girl would learn about marriage issues through the church, newspapers, radio, or informal instruction is very much doubted. The participants at the initiation, that is the *alangizi* (instructors), *angolozole* (monitors, the girls who were initiated earlier and are guiding the new initiates), and others who are usually sponsors, relatives and observers, teach the new initiates about the seriousness of initiation through songs and dancing. In song no. 5, *A Lucy mundipereke*

---

[42] From the survey of 23 girls for example only one girl had parents who came both from the same tribe.

kwa Kawoza, ndikavinire mwana wanga akule, (Lucy take me to Kawoza [a place], that I should initiate my child so that she should grow), urges the parents to take their daughters to listen to instructions at initiation ceremonies. While this song presents the teaching in a more literal way, other songs teach this truth figuratively. For example in song no. 40 *Nkhuku, nkhanga ndi ana* (Chicken, guinea fowl and chicks), the hen and guinea fowl are the *alangizi* and the chicks are the girls to be initiated. The new initiates are challenged in their minds to visualize a hen with her chicks, and be reminded that just as the chicks look to the hen for survival, the girls should also look to the *alangizi* for survival and should listen carefully to the instruction given by the *alangizi*. Apart from figurative expression in the songs, drama is incorporated in the same song no. 40 that teaches the girls' submission to the *alangizi*. The girls continue to move on their buttocks back and forth as the *alangizi* continue to sing the chorus. As long as the chorus is sung, the girls have to perform that action to signify obedience. One could argue that this drama was to draw attention from the girls but because the girls were moving on their buttocks on a very rough ground outside the church, with not much clothing on them, it can also be said that this drama was oppressive and maybe another drama would have been more appropriate, for example if the girls could be made to run around in a circle while the song was sung.

The same predicament was seen in the song that teaches the girls the right procedure for initiation of their future daughters: that they need to go to the chief, to ask for permission to initiate their children. This teaching was done in song no. 59 *Kalambe, kalambe kwa mfumu* (go and ask permission, go and ask permission from the chief). The children had to move on their bottoms over a distance of 10 metres, periodically sitting up as appropriate to the rhythm of the song. While the teaching is important, another drama, which would be more liberating as well as culturally fitting, could have been put in place. For example, it would not be a bad idea to have a woman dressed up in a chiefly attire (after all, in this matrilineal society, to have a woman chief is regular) and be seated on a stool or something and the girls one by one would come and bow to the chief. In terms of internalizing the message, this proposal would be more positive than the former.

The importance of initiation was also taught through drilling the girls with symbols that those who were not initiated would not know. This is appropriate because even Jesus Christ sometimes taught his disciples in parables with the intention that those who were "outside" (not his disciples) would not understand even though they would hear. It is through the knowledge of these secret symbols that those who are not initiated are discovered. In this church *chinamwali* one of the symbols was *"livala"*. *Livala* is the name of a tree, but those who have undergone initiation, when asked what *livala* is, must say that they dig it with sticks and that it is *tsitsi la manda* (the hair of the grave).[43] The girls in each community should be able to know where this tree is because all those who are initiated in the community go to this particular place.[44]

To teach general good behaviour

Under this theme girls as well as women are taught good behaviour towards parents, neighbours and elderly people. As regards to parents, girls are encouraged to take heed of the instructions their parents give them. This is done in songs and sometimes even combined with a drama. The songs are sometimes literal and sometimes figurative requiring reading behind the song to get the meaning. When the meanings are not obvious, they are usually brought out by the *mlangizi* who comments on the song or the drama after the recital of *"kunkhani, kunkhani"* which does not have a meaning but signifies that every one should listen to what she is about to say.

In song no. 37, *Sala, naona mwana mbalame, tiye kumanda kwaitana*, (Sarah, I have seen the child of a bird, lets go to the graveyard) has no obvious meaning although some individual words are known to the reader. However the song teaches that the initiate should listen to the instruction of her parents because if she does not she will regret when

---

[43] Patrick Makondesa, Christian Initiation Rites in Southern Malawi, also mentions the *livala* tree: "While at the camp a masked woman chases the girls to the mountain to pick up firewood. This ceremony is known at *kutola nkhuni*. There they are given instructions for womanhood in their homes. At the mountain the *nankungwi* teaches them with demonstration what they are supposed to do when death occurs in their presence. After this they go back to the shelter. At the shelter a stick of a *livala* tree is put in the middle of the camp. Each girl is then asked to take a part of the *livala* tree and dig out the *livala* branch which was placed in the middle of the camp. They are advised that when they have their first menstruation, they are to drink a concoction made from the *livala* leaves. This concoction is a symbol of fertility to make them able to bear children in future.

[44] Other symbols include a corpse of a boy, a corpse of a mother, a corpse of a girl, which will be discussed later.

her mother dies. The meaning was elaborated by the *mlangizi* as a commentary on the song.

In song no. 72, *Ndithu, ndithu, ndi amako ndithu, ngakhale ukhale ukula thupi* (Indeed, indeed, she is indeed your mother, though you may be stout), the girls are reminded to respect their parents regardless of how their parents look like. Even though in this song, the fatness of the mother is referred to, the song aims at educating the girls to respect their parents even with their inadequacies.

The girls are not only taught to respect their mother but also their father, even though they belong to the mother and the uncle according to this matrilineal society. As regards their dads, they are taught a lesson in a moving drama where they are made to beat the roof of the grass-thatched house to look for rats. This drama is rightly called *kusaka makoswe* (hunting for rats). As the girls beat the roof, *alangizi* periodically shout *uyu khoswe* (here is the rat) but they are only lying. The meaning of this drama is later explained by *alangizi*, that the girls should not go under the house when their father is on top of the roof because in the event that he has a torn pant, the girls may accidentally see his private parts which would not be proper behaviour.

The teaching of respecting their parents is further enriched by telling them the reasons why. In song no. 1 *Nyumba ya mako, uziti odi* (The house of your mother, you must say *odi*) the girls are not told to say "excuse" before going into the house as the song implies but into their mother's bedroom. The reasons are not in the words of the song but are said after the song by the *alangizi*. The reasons are that if the girls went into their parents' bedroom without warning, they might find their parents naked which would be inappropriate for the girls and their parents as well. However, if the girls knocked before entering their parents' bedrooms, their parents would have time to dress up if they were undressed. The fact that there is a provision to teach girls certain truths that are not in the song, is positive to the building in of Christian teaching. It shows that *alangizi* could easily incorporate biblical teachings into the Christianized initiation without sacrificing its credibility.

Girls are advised to respect their parents not only when they are unmarried but after marriage as well. Song no. 36 *Sinoya lero, ndamva kuti amayi amwalira, chipatala cha gulupu,* (Sinoya today, I heard that mother passed away, at Queen Elizabeth Hospital in Blantyre) is aimed at teaching the girls that when their mothers are sick, they should be just as concerned as when their husbands are sick. They should not ignore their parents when they are sick. The song ridicules the girl who ignores the death of her parent but the moment her husband dies, she bitterly complains even contemplating cutting up her private parts which are now no longer useful without him.

The girls are also warned not to be obscene to their parents. This is taught in a song such as no. 20 *"Kadamanja, Kadamanja, kulaula amayi wake"* (Kadamanja insults her mother).

Apart from teaching respect of children towards parents, parents are also taught to respect their children at the same time as they participate in the initiation. In Song no. 21 *Inu amayi, ndi amuna anu, mwandiyetsa chikwakwa chometera* (You mother, with your husband, you have taken me as a slasher), for example, teaches parents not to abuse their children by overburdening them with too many house chores.

The other teaching regards girls' respect towards other elderly people as well. In song no. 6 *Phumbwa kudya kachere, ndiponye bwanji muvi* (the Phumbwa bird is eating the kachere fruit, how do I throw my spear), the girls are taught not to throw stones into a tree when adults are sitting under it. In the same song, they are dissuaded from climbing the tree when elders are sitting under it because they might fall over them by accident. The meaning is not so obvious in the song, and is elaborated through a short commentary from the *alangizi*.

In song no. 56 *Kupempha kwa akulu, ndiyang'ana ndi maso* (The elderly requesting, I see by their eyes), girls are instructed to be sensitive to the needs of the elderly by making their own judgement. As the song was sung, the *alangizi* dramatized possible ways of how an elderly person may look while in need of help. A commentary at the end was also added. Here is a place where a biblical text concerning respect for the elderly could be inserted.[45] This can be done without changing the song because there is nothing evil in the song. It would be a meaningful illustration of the teaching.

---

[45] For example Lev 19:32, Rise in the presence of the aged, show respect for elderly and revere your God; Eph. 6:1 Children obey your parents in the Lord for this is right; Exod. 20:12 Honour your father and mother so that you may live long in the land your God is giving you.

Girls are also taught to respect neighbours. In song no. 17, *A Linly, perekani mtondo wotukwanira* (Linly, send [back] the abusive mortar),[46] the meaning is not in the words of the song, it is behind them. The song teaches that the girls should not sour relationships with their neighbours by not returning something that they borrowed. It is evident from this song that songs that have meanings behind them can be interpreted differently.[47]

But is this experience different from the Christian encounter with a biblical text? Therefore, the fact that different meanings are derived from it does not make the song improper. The most important thing is the themes through the song, whether they match the required teaching.

The girl is also warned not to be envious of her fellow women in a dramatic song no. 28 *Likita, iwe, anzathu olemera, muvala nsalu zambiri* (You Likita, our friends who are rich, you wear many clothes). In this song, the girl who dances takes the role of a rich girl and seems to enjoy that status and shows that this is the status she prefers. However, the lesson in the song is for the poor girl who does not have enough to show off. This is one method of teaching used in initiation where negative actions are used to teach the positive. Is such attempt not resonant with biblical passages such as where although young people are told to enjoy themselves, the lesson is to urge them not to?[48]

To teach girls on taboos and superstitions

In this category the main issues relate to the girls' health. One of the key health issues relates to the dangers of menstrual blood. The initial menstrual blood is handled very cautiously by the society[49] to protect the girl from infertility and witchcraft. For this reason, the girls are told that this

---

[46] See also Patrick Makondesa, "Christian Initiation Rites in Southern Malawi", which has a similar song (no. 39): "Khwikire pereka mtondo wotukanira (Give back quickly the captivating mortar). Meaning: When you borrow somebody's property give it back before he or she begins to complain.".

[47] This is why the meanings in the songs and those recorded on the cassette sometimes differ.

[48] For example Eccl 11:9 "Be happy, young man, while you are young, and let your heart give you joy in the days of your youth. Follow the ways of your heart and whatever your eyes see, but know that for all these things God will bring you to judgement."

[49] Among the Chewa it is a sign of age and hope for continuation of the society. Isabel Phiri, *Women, Presbyterianism and Patriarchy*, p. 14.

menstrual blood has to be buried by the *alangizi* only. They are the ones who can protect them from any form of witchcraft.[50] This is done by burying all the things used by the girl that were in touch with menstrual blood, in a secret place, usually under a tree. If these things were not properly buried, the girl would be infertile as witches might get her menstrual blood materials and use them to bewitch her. This is expressed in song number 79: *Watola mphande, watola mphande ya manja* (you have taken monthly period linen, monthly period linen of the hands.) Although the song does not make enough sense it teaches that if the monthly period linen is not buried properly, the owner can suffer from *chikawo*,[51] a disease similar to *tsempho* or others can use the linen to bewitch the girl.

The dangers of menstrual blood bringing disease and death to men is taught in songs. In song 77 *Chinyela chitha amuna, akazi nasala* (*Chinyela* [name of a disease] kills the men and leaves the women), the girls are taught not to have sex during their menstrual period.[52] The instructors also take time to educate the girls thoroughly on how they can recognize the point when the menstruation period is over and they are again ready to have sexual relations.[53]

What is interesting in the disease known as *chinyela*[54] is that the symptoms given for the disease are synonymous to those given for HIV/AIDS. The patient with *chinyela* experiences hair loss, lack of appetite, fever and likes to sit in the sun. The only difference is that, traditionally, *chinyela* is perceived to be curable through traditional herbs. It is therefore difficult for the rural people to identify sufferers of HIV/AIDS in their communities because of the possibility that they may be *chinyela* patients. This is also where Baptist women should insert a teaching that

---

[50]   See *chinamwali* document in the appendix.
[51]   J.W.M. van Breugel, *Chewa Traditional Religion*, Blantyre: CLAIM-Kachere, 2001, p. 166, refers to this disease as *mdulo*.
[52]   See also Renata Sakaike, Collection of Materials, Nsondo Rite, p. 2.
[53]   Also in other traditional initiation like *nsondo*. See Renata Sakaike, "Collection of Materials, Nsondo Rite", University of Malawi, 1996, p. 2; Patrick Makondesa "Christian Initiation Rites in Southern Malawi," MA Module 1, Department of Theology and Religious Studies, 1999, p. 13. Makondesa gives a song to this effect that says "Linly ukaona magazi ku nyini usathire mchere udzatupitsa anthu pamudzi" means "Linly when you see blood from the vagina do not put salt in relish, you will make people swollen in the village." Ngoni Women are not supposed to put salt into relish. In this church *chinamwali* this was not taught and if done, it is taught outside this setting.
[54]   In other cases the word used is Kanyela.

will educate women on the Christian perspective on menstrual blood and the realities of HIV/AIDS in the communities.[55] This would liberate women to have sexual relations during the menstruation period if they so desire. In fact, they should also be told of some of the advantages of having sex during the menstruation period such as, that it is the time when some women desire to have sex, and that it is a time when one is unable to conceive and therefore good for those using natural methods as a means of birth control.

Some of the teachings on taboos are indeed nonsense, as Europeans define that. This concerns the superstitious teaching given to the girls. In the *chinamwali cha litiwo* (initiation for women with first pregnancy), for example, the weaving of sisal into a rope to be used for the prevention of miscarriage seems to be useless, unless somehow some chemicals in this sisal, through body fluids are able to seep through the skin and interfere with the process of pregnancy. Even if that was the case, the dramatization of how to weave the sisal while the women stands only on one leg for more than 30 minutes seems to be ridiculous.

The other superstitious teaching in the same initiation concerns the anointing of the pregnant women with castor oil on her forehead. This tradition is called *chipendo*. The oil is supposed to run vertically straight across her navel towards her vagina if she was not unfaithful at the conception of her pregnancy. This superstition goes on to say that if there were a woman who commits adultery with the husband of this woman at the place of the anointing, the woman would loose her pregnancy at the same time. This is known as *chivuwa*. This seems to be very unlikely. Probably, the central theme in this tradition is that of faithfulness. Baptist women can easily add a biblical lesson on faithfulness in marriage and its advantages in the prevention of HIV and AIDS. These women should challenge the initiate that instead of loosing pregnancy because of unfaithfulness on the part of the husband, the woman and the child including her husband can contract HIV.

Other similar lessons on culture concern the use of herbs to protect oneself from witchcraft. At the beginning of initiation it is the concern of the *alangizi* to make sure that the initiates are firmly protected from witchcraft attacks. This is why a special herbal mixture is made by the

---

[55] Another danger is that, since *chinyela* is conceived as killing but easily curable, HIV/AIDS may be considered as possessing the same qualities.

alangizi to be given to the pastor and the pastor's wife, so that they are protected from such forces. In the church where initiation begins, fire made out of traditional herbs to chase away evil spirits is made in the centre of the church for the same purpose.

The theme of using traditional medicine to fight against evil is even seen during the dramatization and singing at the corpse of a mother who was neglected by her girl child.[56] At this juncture the *alangizi* demonstrate how knowledge of a very powerful traditional medicine helps the witches to excel in their witchcraft pursuits.[57]

This is shown by drama as those witches with less powerful traditional herbs fail to take the corpse home. Additionally, the girls are introduced to several kinds of traditional medicines in the form of leaves that they will need for protection against witchcraft. Baptist women can take advantage here to talk about how a Christian girl can live a victorious life over powers of darkness. This is where a passage such as Ephesians 6:10-18 about having the full armour of God can be appropriate.

Some of the African Traditional Religion teachings are not understood by the majority. This was seen during the *chinamwali choweramira ana*. There were many symbolisms such as dancing with embers of fire, and swinging them around, which were not understood by the observers. Such activities can as well be left out in the pursuit of inculturation, because, how can the church inculturate something that is hardly understood by them?

No teaching, just entertainment

Although initiation is aimed at educating girls, some of the songs and activities do not mean anything. This is as regards these songs: song no. 11, *Njamajo, ajanyama* that cannot be translated literally; song no. 19, *Bongololo waduka mutu, nati akalume,* (the millipede has lost its head, he wanted to go and bite.)[58] And no. 31, *Akachitole ndi nkhongo, akachisiye ndi nkhongo,* (she should go and pick it with the back of the head, she should leave it with the back of her head). The activities of the latter

---

[56] See songs 51, 52 and 53 in *chinamwali* document in the appendix.
[57] Women leaders of Zomba *Umodzi* Association also admitted this (20.3.2001).
[58] This seems to me to be a song about not having sex when menstruating. See Patrick Makondesa, Christian Initiation Rites in Southern Malawi, "*Bongololo waduka mutu nati alume.*" (A millipede lost its head when he wanted to bite) is explained as "a man can prepare to have sex with his wife, only to be told she is menstruating."

song were painful as the girls had to twist their heads while lying on their back to get a stick under their backs. Since the song does not have an obvious meaning, it is difficult to suggest ways of how Baptist women could inculturate this part. My only guess is that this latter song teaches girls to work hard, but if this is right, this lesson could be done without such painful actions. Songs and activities that do not have any meaning should not necessary be removed from the initiation. They are an important segment of entertainment.

To teach marriage issues

As has been shown above, it is wrong to say that initiation is only intended for sexual education. There are other lessons as well covered in this programme. Nevertheless, the bulk of the initiation teaching is related to marriage, and more so, to sex education. Some of the specific areas of sex education taught in this church *chinamwali* were as follows:

Time to have sex

Girls are dissuaded to have premarital sex. This lesson is brought to the girls in a dramatic way.[59] The girls, as they go into the bush, suddenly find a corpse of a dead girl well covered by cloth.[60] Near the corpse are women wailing and crying, mentioning the name of the girl who has died. The new initiates cannot resist the urge to cry, and they cry bitterly. After a while, the *alangizi* command everyone to stop crying and song no. 48 is sung: *Mtsikana woyendayenda, anafera panjira, mwana wachigololo, anafera pa njira* (the moving [promiscuous] girl, she died on the way, the fornicious child died on the road).

After the song was sung, while others clapped hands, the *mlangizi* gave her commentary on the drama to the initiates. She told the initiates that the girl died because she was immoral. She was never afraid of sleeping with men including those much older than her. She then cautioned the initiates never to involve themselves in premarital sex because they could contract AIDS and die leaving their parents in poverty. This teaching is contrary to the frequent perception that initiation ceremonies

---

[59] See *chinamwali* document in the appendix.
[60] The name of the dead girl is known as *"anafera panjira"* (she died along the road). Ibid.

encourage immorality in girls.[61] If the perception is true, then this is where the church has excelled to leave that negative teaching and place emphasis on teaching against fornication and adultery. This is a relevant teaching especially in this crucial era of the AIDS endemic, and it is encouraging to see that even this teaching of AIDS prevention is included at this point.

The same lesson against premarital sex and adultery was taught when the initiates were being taught about respecting their fathers at a drama known as *kusaka makoswe* (looking for rats).[62] This also shows that a drama, a song or any action during initiation may have more than one lesson. At this drama of *kusaka makoswe*, the teaching against immorality was not in the drama or the songs, it was given in the *alangizi's* a commentary on the drama.

Girls are also taught about the right time to have sex when they are married. This is because even when they are married, they cannot have sex each time they want. They are prohibited to have sex during menstruation as discussed before, but also during certain events. When the child is sick, they are not to have sex. This teaching is done through songs. Song no. 38 *Gagadila, chisoni amuna, mwana natodwala iye nandiitana bwera tigagadile ga* (Have sex, sorry [my] husband, the child is sick, he calls me: come, let us have sex): *Gagadila* is not a Chewa word, it is just an idiom and here it is refers to having sex. The song teaches the girls that when the child is sick and their husbands asks them for sex, they should refuse. In the traditional belief, some diseases such as measles are perceived to worsen through sexual relations of the parents.[63]

It is intriguing that certain prohibitions about when to have sex between husband and wife were not included in this church *chinamwali*. Such prohibitions include when to resume sex after delivery as dis-

---

[61] Renata Sakaike shows the involvement of *fisi* in the initiation and shows how this is cherished by one of the interviewees in his research. See Renata Sakaike "Collection of Materials" p. 2 and Patrick Makondesa also gives this impression in the songs, such as this: *Pamene paja pangotalika ine ndinafikapo.* (The distance is just very far, but I reached there myself.) Meaning: When you had access to sexual intercourse with a certain woman do not boast and publicize it. This will destroy the woman's dignity. See Patrick Makondesa Christian Initiation Rites in Southern Malawi.
[62] This drama was already explained earlier.
[63] On this and related reasons for sexual abstention see, J.W.M. van Breugel, *Chewa Traditional Religion*, Blantyre: CLAIM-Kachere, 2001, pp. 203-207.

cussed in chapter 3 regarding *kutenga mwana*[64] and also not to have sex when the couple has a baby who is still breastfeeding. The parents can only have sex when the baby is on the same mat where the parents are having sex. If they have sex in the absence of the baby, the baby will die.

Omission of such prohibitions in the initiation ceremony which included all the four major stages of initiation in a woman's life shows that not every belief and practice Baptist women adhere to, can be traced through initiation ceremonies. This suggests that even in this matrilineal culture where communal initiation rites are emphasized there are other rites done privately. It is not convincing that such omissions were done because it was a Christianized initiation because even in the traditional initiation such teachings seem to be absent.[65]

Satisfaction in sex

On this subject, it is clear that lessons are more on women satisfying men during sex than men satisfying women. However, it can be argued, that it is insufficient to gauge whether men are less taught about how they could satisfy women basing on the initiation ceremony of girls, because men do have their own initiation, where they are also taught on how to satisfy women.[66]

In this Christianized initiation rite, girls are taught a dance which involves shaking their waists while standing which is meant to help them satisfy men during sex. This is the main theme from the start of the initiation to the end. As most songs are sung, women dance this dance to teach the initiates the required dance during sex. The thoroughness of the new initiates' dance shows that girls do not learn to dance this dance during this communal initiation rite, but that by the time they come for this communal initiation, they had been already taught the dance privately by the *angolozole* (monitors, girls who were already initiated and have been

---

[64] For *Kutenga Mwana* see Rachel Nyagondwe Banda, *Women of Bible and Culture*, pp. 103-104. However song no. 12, *Mbuziyi, muli atonde* (This goat, you are a male goat) teaches husbands to wait for the wife to recover from delivery wounds before resuming sex with her, but does not talk about the rituals surrounding *kutenga mwana*.

[65] One of them is the elongation of the *labia minora*, another the sexual dance.

[66] Isabel Phiri argues that boys are not taught such. See Isabel Phiri, *Women, Presbyterianism and Patriarchy*, p. 40.

assigned to teach the girls to dance).[67] This private teaching is done usually in the evening.

The significance of the dance is also taught through songs. An example is song no. 47, *Mayi, zinthu zanga zanyekulira* (mother, my things are assisting in sex). It is hard to come up with an exact translation of *zanyekulira* because this word is also figurative. However the meaning of the song is to teach the initiates that when they have sex with a man, it is the swerving of the waist like in winnowing that helps the man to enjoy sex. This dance has often been condemned as evil and in other Christianized initiations like in the *Buku la Alangizi* initiation, this dance is left out. But is it not true that such dancing is helpful in sexual intercourse? If this is the case then the church should consider a way of teaching girls this dance before marriage as it is done in this particular church initiation. Some may argue that this dance should be taught just before marriage but it is easier to master the dance while one is young than when one is older. In any case, the dance is taught before puberty and since the sexual hormones are not active at this time, the child is able to learn the dance well without attaching feelings to it.

The dance is not of one type, there are several versions and all show the possible alternatives a girl can use to satisfy the man in sex but also to add variety to sex. However, although there are varieties in the dance, any dance, which does not properly swerve the waist, is discouraged. It is interesting that the western ways of dancing are also encroaching on the tradition. At this particular initiation, a girl who had been sent for initiation by her parents who live in town was able to combine her town dance (dancing with shoulders) and the traditional dance and became a centre of attraction.

Sex techniques

Apart from dancing, girls are oriented as to the different positions they should assume to give variety to sex.[68] In song 34 *A Nyundo kubedi kuja mumatotani kukada? Ndimangotere!* (Mr Nyundo, on your bed, when it is dark, what do you do? I just do like this). The sex technique is not in the

---

[67] Confirmed by the twenty-three girls interviewed.

[68] Lessons on sex techniques are not unique to this *chinamwali*. For example song no 23 in Makondesa's text: *Anyamata a kwa Khoviwa amachinda ngati mtambo,* meaning some men are not good at lovemaking. See Patrick Makondesa, "Christian Initiation Rites in Southern Malawi," p. 13.

song; it is in how the girls dance, when they sing, "I just do like this!" This is why knowledge of songs as such is not enough to learn about initiation. To get the full story, one must participate in it. As the girls danced this song, several ways of dancing were demonstrated.

Some of the techniques are explained in a song, so that girls have a picture of what happens during sex. One of such songs is no. 33: *Tete ... mwendo uli kukhoma wina uli kubedi, abale ndikokeleni kukhonde?* ([tete is an ideophone?]) one leg at the wall, the other on the bed, friends take me to the verandah) tells the initiates that although they are dancing as standing, sex is also done while lying down, and sometimes requires that legs should be in the position described in the song.

In addition, when in a lying position, the girl is taught the different functions of her body during sex. This is well explained in song no. 34 *Jejemera, mutu wako umagwera, bere lako ilo pilo, mimba yako ndi matilesi, chiuno chako chimagwedera, chinena chikatota* (your breast is the pillow [of your husband], your stomach is the mattress, your waist is for swerving, your vagina, take it [the penis] in).

Apart from the technique, the girl is taught on what to expect during sex. The girls are taught that they might shiver (*jejemera*) as in song no. 34 above. And also that they will actually desire to have sex as in song no. 30, *Chikuni chakolera* (The firewood has caught fire). This phrase does not refer to wood but to sexual feelings being aroused.

The girl is also prepared mentally on what to expect when the man is ready for sex. She is told about the change in the size of his penis due to the erection. This is explained not in a drama but in a song such as song no. 26, *Hinawone, Mbolo nayigwa ...* (I have never seen, the penis falling....). This phrase is a figurative expression to refer to erection. This is an example of the areas where some feel uncomfortable with initiation because of the mentioning of the private parts of the body. But recognizing that this is done in the context of women only, the criticism may be unfounded. If God created everything beautiful, there is nothing to be ashamed of if it is done in the proper context. It would be improper if these body parts were mentioned in the presence of men, except one's husband.[69]

---

[69] As such, I commend the attempt in the *Buku la Alangizi* to teach the anatomy of the girl as proper and I doubt that blatant language of mentioning body parts would discourage Baptist women to send their children for Christianized initiation. Learning about functions of the body is important to girls in Baptist churches in this region be-

Making choices

Girls are taught to marry boys who have gone through initiation because then they would enjoy sex more. In song 29 *Mkoko wa nthochi siuchedwa kulemera* (The banana bunch becomes tired quickly), is an analogy used to teach girls that if they marry uninitiated boys, they would not be satisfied during sex. Such boys would easily get tired before their women got satisfied. However, girls are told that they should be free to choose what kind of initiation they prefer. This lesson is taught in songs such as song no. 8; *Katcha zili mu Malomwe, wajando, wazoto, machende achepe*, (Katcha [ideophone] are with the Lomwe, those who have gone through *jando*, through *zoto*, the testicles should be small). *Wachilomwe* refers to boys who are initiated but are not circumcised, *wajando* refers to boys who are circumcised; *wazoto*, refers to boys who are initiated but got only a partial circumcision:[70] This teaching is liberative because it implies that the girls can make choices. However, it can be oppressive if the girl loves a man who is not initiated and she is denied the chance to marry him.

Labia minora

Opinions on the role of the *labia minora* in relation to sex are twofold. Some cultures promote the removal of the *labia minora*[71] while some promote their lengthening.[72] In the former practice, the *labia minora* are

---

cause most of them are rural, and only a few make it to Secondary School where such a subject is taught. See also Isabel Phiri, *Women, Presbyterianism and Patriarchy*, p. 58.
[70] This explanation is on the cassette. For further explanation of *Zoto, Jando* see J.C. Chakanza, "The Unfinished Agenda: Puberty Rites and the Response of the Roman Catholic Church in Southern Malawi, 1901-1994", p. 3.
[71] See for example, Martin Mgeni, "Girls Initiation in a Yao Setting and Christian Attitude, p. 1. In this he states that the reduction of the *labia minora* was originally done with a sharp knife known as *chisondo* from where the name *nsondo* rite is derived. He also shows how this way of reducing labia minora has been replaced by the drinking of herbal medicine known as *nsondoka*. Renata Sakaike also shows this and among the Yao where she did research, the herbal medicine used is *chipembere*. See Renata Sakaike, Collection of Materials, Nsondo Rite, 1996, p. 2.
[72] For example Sakaike shows this in the *chiputu* rite. See Renata Sakaike, Collection of Materials, Nsondo Rite, p. 2; See also J.C. Chakanza, "The Unfinished Agenda: Puberty Rites and the Response of the Roman Catholic Church in Southern Malawi".

removed either through circumcision or the drinking of traditional medicine so that the man does not have a hindrance to quick penetration during sex. The practice to lengthen the *labia minora* is not clear but seems to revolve around the husband being able to play with them during sex. In this Christianized initiation, the lengthening of the *labia minora* was encouraged, though reasons were not given. And in fact song no. 23 *Ndinapita kwa bwenzi langa, bwenzi langa anandifunsa, zonsezi ndi zako?* (I went to my boyfriend, my boyfriend asked me, are all these yours?), shows that some men are even surprised at the existence of long *labia minora* that are naturally not supposed to be such. On the other hand, the question the boyfriend asks may imply that he is flattered with such long *labia minora* and this is the understanding the girls are given in this church initiation.

In song no. 43, *Ndiuzeni, nyini ya nkhuku* (tell me, the vagina of the hen) it is figuratively demonstrated to the girls how to lengthen the *labia minora* (*kuthuna/kukoka*). This is done by showing them the vagina of the chicken. It is not clear whether the girls really got the message during this demonstration. The real lesson seems clearly to be given privately and by the time girls come for this communal initiation, they already have lengthened the *labia minora* or are working on it.[73] The disagreement on the usage of *labia minora* during sex should not imply that the lengthening of *labia minora* is not important. The church should encourage this because there are testimonies that this indeed does contribute to stability in marriage.[74]

The climax of sex education is the drama of the corpse of a boy while the girls are in the bush. In song 58 *Kalulu kulumpha njira* (Hare jumping the road), the meaning is obscure, but during the commentary, the girls were told that they need to respect men who are impotent and cannot have an erection to have sex. What was impressive was the reference the *mlangizi* made that they should love such as they love themselves according to the Bible. She also talked about God creating some men in

---

[73] Interviews of the twenty three girls indicated this.

[74] Among the Amang'anja in the *chiputu* initiation girls are taught that a man plays with them and that they arouse a man for sex. See Renata Sakaike, Collection of Materials, Nsondo Rite, p. 3. Chakanza shows the common perception that lack of elongation of labia minora encourages divorce. See J.C. Chakanza, "The Unfinished Agenda: Puberty Rites and the Response of the Roman Catholic Church in Southern Malawi," p. 4.

this way and that they must be respected as such. She ended the teaching of respecting the impotent in a drama phrase *ngati Mulungu sanampatse chochindira, chochindira amapatsa ndani?* (If God hasn't given him a penis that can have an erection, who will give it to him?)

Submission to the husband

Apart from lessons related to sex education, girls are taught concerning submission to their husbands. In song 28 for example *Likita iwe, anzathu olemera* (Likita, our friends who are rich), the initiates are taught to be contented with what they have. They are told not to ask for a dress from their husbands if they need one.

Song no. 49 *Mwana mnyamata usagone, utagona? Ona dina, tandileke. Ndamwa mowa* (Young man, do not sleep, are you sleeping? See my vagina. Leave me alone, I drank beer) can well be interpreted to mean that the husband is stupid for denying his wife sexual pleasure. But this song is interpreted to mean that the girls are not to request sex, rather that the girls should wait for their husbands to request it. This is where the church can bring in the Christian teaching that the husband is not alone in charge of his sexuality,[75] without removing the song. During the time of commentary by the *mlangizi*, biblical verses on sharing in a family and the fact that the owner of the men's body is the woman and vice versa can be included.[76]

Girls are also taught to condone immorality of their husbands. This is very dangerous, especially with the AIDS epidemic. In song no. 64, *Tsegulire, ndakana, apanja, mulibe mwambo,* (Open for me, I have refused, those outside have no behaviour, those in the house, you do not have behavior), the girls are taught that if their husband sleeps outside, and comes very late at night they should not refuse him to come into the house because "an animal could kill him". They are also dissuaded to be

---

[75] 1 Corinthians 7:3-5: "The husband should fulfill his marital duty to his wife, and likewise the wife to her husband. The wife's body does not belong to her alone but also to her husband. In the same way, the husband's body does not belong to him alone but also to his wife. Do not deprive each other except by mutual consent and for a time, so that you may devote yourselves to prayer. Then come together again so that Satan will not tempt you because of your lack of self-control.".
[76] An example would be Eph 5:28-29: "In this same way, husbands ought to love their wives as their own bodies. He who loves his wife loves himself. After all, no one ever hated his own body, but he feeds and cares for it, just as Christ does the church."

jealous with their husbands. Baptist women should recognize the problem with this song and instead of teaching girls to condone promiscuity, they should teach them the importance of communication and faithfulness in marriage and educate them on how to defend their rights which includes prevention of HIV infection through faithfulness. This also can be done without removing or even changing the song.

Behaviour of wife to husband

Girls are also taught how to behave in the presence of their husbands. They are taught that they need to be decent in the eyes of the public but not when they are on their own with their husbands. During this time, she should not even bother how she positions her legs when sitting. Let her husband see her private parts if possible. This is taught in a dramatic song and dance no. 27, *Munyumba mwa amayi mukhale mulitsitsa, munyumba mwa amuna anu mukhale mulivekete* (In your mother's house sit decently, but in your husband's house sit anyhow even with legs thrown in the air). The girls obviously enjoyed the dance because they danced this song for about half an hour while throwing their legs up in the most awkward positions. It is clear that the wife, although she cannot ask sex from her husband verbally, can do it by actions such as her "indecent" sitting in his presence. The church can develop this theme and include other ways of how a woman can be attractive to her husband such as through cleanliness, and also not with outward adornment alone but with a quiet spirit among other Christian virtues for a married woman.[77]

Cleanliness

The new initiates are taught how they can sweep their houses. This is done in a drama where the *alangizi* demonstrate how to sweep the house, for example in song no. 66, *Nyanyuwe, sesele namwali,* (Nyanyuwe [name] sweep girl [initiate], sweep for me). As this song was sung, the *alangizi* swept the floor as an example to the initiates. The girls

---

[77] 1 Peter 3:3: "Your beauty should not come from outward adornment, such as braided hair and the wearing of gold jewelry and fine clothes. Instead, it should be that of your inner self, the unfading beauty of a gentle and quiet spirit, which is of great worth in God's sight.".

were also told not to sweep when there are people around, as that would be a sign of disrespect.

The initiates were not only taught about cleaning their homes but also their bodies. Generally, the girls were taught to pay attention to washing their private parts, not just face and head. In song no. 75, *Nanchengwa, usamba mutu, uleka uku*, (Nanchengwa [a girl's name], you wash your head, [but] there you leave out). This lesson is also conveyed through drama as the song is sung.

Another major area of cleanliness concerns taking care of the monthly period linen. In song no. 67, *Machakala ndataye kuti? Taya khonde* (Where do I throw the monthly period linen? Throw it on the verandah), the girls are taught not to dry this linen where people might see it. This is taught through negative actions in a drama. As the above song is sung, the linen is thrown in different places where it is not supposed to be, for example, on the dining table, on the door outside frame, on top of the plate and the like. And indeed the mood is filled with laughter and drama-tized negative reaction of the initiates as to why the girl would be so un-wise as to place her linen in those places.

The girls are then taught how to dry their linen properly. The *mlangizi* demonstrates this by tying a string around her waist. She washes the dirty linen and fixes it onto a string at the side. She takes the dry linen and shows how to fit it so that it will catch the blood flow. The demonstra-tion of how to fit in the linen was also very entertaining when the *mlangizi* showed how it is not supposed to be done, such as letting it protrude at one's back, to be seen by people.

On the same subject, girls are taught not to wash the monthly period linen in the kitchen utensils. This is considered as unclean and could contaminate food. They are also dissuaded from using the same utensils with their mothers when washing the linen. This was taught through song no. 70, *Choyenda ndi ana, ndalapa lero, mwana machakala, salala mbi-yamu*, (To go with children, I have stopped today, the monthly period linen ... Walking with children, I will not do it again, she leaves her monthly period linen in my pot). The church does not necessarily have to condemn such lessons, because, although it is nothing wrong for the daughter and the mother to use the same pot for washing, it is not an unchristian practice, and it can be left as it is.

Medical

Though initiation ceremonies are considered to be traditional, it is amazing that they do contain right medical advice to the girls. However some of the medical advice is purely suspicion or even wrong. An example of wrong medical advice to the girls is as regards the danger of menstrual blood as discussed earlier.

Some of the right medical lessons were concerning delivery of the baby during *litiwo*. The initiates are told the signs that the woman should observe when she is about to deliver. This is done in song as well as drama. In song no. 15, *Kuwotcha, akukanga, kutanda unya manyi mwana, asanatuluke, uyamba kusanza,* (To feel hot, she is failing, you produce stool before the child comes out, you start vomiting before the child comes out), the women are taught what they should expect before the child is born. Although not all women may feel all the signs mentioned in the song, the signs are medically correct and are experienced by some women. The women are also taught that delivery takes a long time and the onset of labour pains does not necessarily mean that the child is nearly coming. This lesson was expressed in song no. 16, *Chitetete, zuwali, zuwali, kukalowa, zuwa ndi kutuluka,* (Nothing is done, this sun, this sun, to go and set, the sun comes out). Although the full meaning is not in the song, through the drama and commentary, the girls are taught that sometimes a woman can wait for a child to be born from morning to sunset, for this reason they need to be patient. This lesson is true, but the danger is that women are also taught to wait at home and go to the hospital only when the signs such as vomiting have started. This is dangerous as the baby might be born before reaching the hospital, because not all women experience vomiting before the child comes. This is especially dangerous if it is a complicated delivery, this can endanger both the mother and the child.

The other medical lesson was during the young girls' initiation at the place where they encountered the corpse of the mother. Apart from issues relating to ATR, girls were taught how they could recognize that someone is dying. This was done through singing song no. 54, *Ndiuzeni njira ya kumanda* (Tell me the way of the grave). Through the guidance of the *alangizi*, the girls were told that a person begins to die from the feet going up to the head and that the body will loose heat in this direction.

Behaviour in a community

Under this topic, girls were taught not to be obscene. At a ceremony known as *chikwatu*[78] the children were told not to catch a chicken and play with it in the presence of parents. They were also discouraged from insulting chicken in the presence of the elders. It may be surprising as to why insults towards this particular animal are discouraged. This is because a chicken is used at initiation for instruction and therefore someone who has been to an initiation camp should not just talk about it anyhow.

Similarly, girls are warned against talking about *madeya* (maize husks) in the presence of their brothers. This prohibition is also related to the use of *madeya* during initiation and the meanings attached to it. *Madeya* is used at a ceremony known as *ozinyera* (someone who is dirty).[79] Apart from using this ceremony to teach girls to clean the elderly when they are dirty, *madeya* is a symbol referring to a boy who is not circumcised, so to talk about *madeya* in the presence of their brothers is to imply that they are not circumcised.

The girls are also taught against stealing and insulting others. This is taught in songs and one of the songs is no. 4 *Chokuba musiye pompano* (stealing, stop now). These values are also part and parcel of the Christian message. Baptist women can therefore capitalize on them by even referring to the Bible.

The girls are it also warned against bad behaviour through scaring them with masked women who pretend to be pigs. This was done when they went into the bush. As the initiates were moving ahead, these women acting like pigs suddenly came from the river with hoes in their hands. The new initiates cried profusely but were stopped by the *alangizi* and the *angolozole*. The idea was to scare them against rudeness.[80]

---

[78] See *chinamwali* document in the appendix.
[79] Ibid.
[80] Ibid.

Baptist *chinamwali*

Church chinamwali *has an edge over the booklet* chinamwali

The booklet *chinamwali* has received no or nearly no support among the Baptist women of Southern Malawi. In the South East region for example, there are cases where an attempt to use the booklet has been made, but the response has been unsatisfactory to warrant its continued usage. In Tambala Baptist in Jali for example, it was used only once and at that particular time only one girl registered for initiation. Because of lack of patronage, the church no longer uses the booklet for initiation. The other reason for lack of usage in the churches is because Baptist churches unlike CCAP and Catholics, where such attempts have succeeded, do not rely on the dictates of a central church government. Each congregation is free to choose what is seen to be relevant to it. In Baptist churches, initiation ceremonies are not doctrinal and are left to the discretion of the individual consciences of participants and to the choices of local congregations. This is why, even though the Westers spelt out their stand on traditional dances, it was only applicable to the moment when one made a decision to join the church, thereafter, a Baptist woman had to be allowed to exercise her own individual conscience, whether or not to participate in traditional initiation.

In the earlier period, one *mlangizi* was responsible for organizing initiation ceremonies for girls in several Baptist congregations. In the South East region these were usually pastors' wives who were also chiefs' wives. However, even though they were Baptist women leaders, the type of *chinamwali* they conducted was basically a traditional *chinamwali*. This was possible because there was no supervision from the missionaries, as in other Christianized initiations.

Mrs Wester, for example, did not attend the ceremonies, so it was difficult to control the proceedings at the ceremonies and even to have a chance to assess their relevance to the women's faith and their role in church and society. Nevertheless, the introduction of the *ulangizi* booklet suggests that missionary women as well as some locals were suspicious of the activities of the initiation ceremonies. The booklet was designed to help control the teachings at the initiation ceremonies. The positive thing about the booklet *chinamwali* is that it introduced the concept of having initiation teaching in a church building. However women in the South

East region have seen that the *Alangizi* booklet is not relevant to them. Therefore, they have decided to construct their own *chinamwali* in the church without interference or assistance from the missionaries. Although this *chinamwali* is slowly being adopted by congregations, and lacks proper organisation, there is evidence that this is the alternative the Baptist women in Southern Malawi want to have rather than the booklet *chinamwali*.

The credibility of booklet chinamwali

Although the booklet provides opportunities to teach girls the Bible such as by its inclusion of Ps 139:13-14 and 1 Cor 6:19-20, for teaching against premarital sex, and verses relating to how one can be saved,[81] and teaches the anatomy of the girls, it has inherent problems that make it unacceptable among the Baptists in this region.[82]

The major problem lies with its approach. Firstly, it rejects payment of a fee to the instructors, a necessary incentive in the traditional initiation. This is possibly why in many local churches, although instructors (*alangizi*) are elected, they are not active. Secondly its starts with instructions for girls who have reached puberty. Although this is adequate in some places such as the Northern region where initiation of girls begins at that stage,[83] it leaves out the important initiation of young girls before puberty that is much supported in Southern Malawi. Thirdly, its method of teaching that excludes drama, singing, dancing, clapping of hands, figurative language, symbolism, among other things, reduces the initiation to dullness and hence it is less appealing to girls who might desire to be initiated in Southern Malawi. Although this booklet includes instruction of stages of initiation such as delivery, puberty and marriage, it lacks interaction with cultural teachings in the traditional *chinamwali*, which are not necessarily against these women's faith. When initiating girls concerning delivery for example, preparation for delivery such as position in delivery and pointers to delivery time are excluded. The initiation begins at the

---

[81] See *Buku la Alangizi*, pp. 2-3.
[82] In some Baptist churches in the Central Region the booklet is used regularly as the only means for the girls' initiation, which last only an hour or so, and which seem to be not very impressive (Information from Molly Longwe, 12.2000).
[83] Makhaza Sylvester Saukani Phiri, Puberty Rites for Girls in Mlefu-Mbemba Village in Traditional Authority Mzukuzuku at Embangweni in South Mzimba, BEd, Department of Theology and Religious Studies, 2001, p. 6.

time when the baby is born. Additionally, the qualifications for selection of an instructor are only based on Christian commitment and disregard cultural qualifications for an instructor and hence grassroots people cannot trust the validity of such instructors. In the traditional setup it is important that they should have gone through a particular initiation before they can instruct others. In the booklet, qualifications of an instructor exclude this and merely demand a woman who is a Christian, married, with a child and able to read and write. Although these are important ingredients, due to the fact that these women did not go for initiation, the society would not respect their teachings.

Further, the booklet is consumed by the desire to make converts to Christ among the girls. Although this is central to the Baptist faith, what is central to initiation is that the girls should be changed into adults. Initiation, therefore, is about teaching the girls aspects of life in the society that are perceived to make a girl grow to adulthood. Therefore the message of conversion should not be the driving force in the initiation programme.

The other weakness is the disregard of the usage of symbols in the booklet *chinamwali*. In the Christianized initiation some of them could be removed because they are based on superstition, which is not in line with the Christian faith unless they are combined with a biblical teaching as regards such an old tradition. An example is the symbol of *livala* and indeed I likewise could not understand a thing although the drama of the digging with the sticks and dancing of the girls was very impressive. It is interesting that apart from the fact that the meaning of this symbol is hidden, that hidden meaning varies. Some interpret it as making girls fertile after digging this tree but for the majority it is just meant to distinguish the initiated from the non-initiated girls if they are able to explain the meaning. But the inclusion of symbols in the booklet *chinamwali* would have enhanced its credibility.

However the majority of symbols were during the initiation known as *kuweramira ana* (bowing for children), which is an initiation for mothers who have grandchildren and have gone through the initiation called *chisimba* (initiation for women who are expecting their first child).[84]

However some of the symbols could be either retained in a Christianized initiation because they do have good teaching, or can be adapted to

---

[84] Even if they never had it but had children, they may go through *kuweramira ana*.

give a more biblical teaching. Such adjustments would be possible and attempts to this effect were already visible in the church *chinamwali* as discussed later. At a certain time during this initiation for example, after the *alangizi* sang song no. 87, she explained to the participants that she did not do some of the things in the initiation because she believed that Christians should refer to the Bible and Jesus in their teaching.

From this critique it is evident that the producers of the booklet *chinamwali* did not have enough dialogue with these women's culture as regards initiation, and although the booklet seems to work elsewhere, (at least somehow) such as in Lilongwe urban churches,[85] a better Christianized initiation should be developed, and not just one that would be used in congregations throughout Malawi, but a particular Christianized initiation for each different cultural grouping depending on the modes of traditional initiation in those communities. The fact that Elizabeth Njolomole from the Central region wrote much of the book,[86] raises the possibility that she was not aware of the traditions in Southern Malawi and may therefore have been ineffective in inculturating initiation rites there. This explains why women in Southern Malawi have adopted their own Christianized initiation, which has won far greater support than the *Buku la Alangizi* initiation.

Church *chinamwali* in the South East region is therefore a better attempt to Christianize initiation rites for the girls in this region, as compared to booklet *chinamwali*, even though there are traces of oppression in it. This is why the church should further develop it and come up with a Christianized initiation that will adequately be inculturated to their Christian message and win support from the majority of grassroots people.[87]

---

[85] Molly Longwe, From *Chinamwali* to *Chilangizo*: the Christianization of Pre-Christian Chewa Initiation Rites in the Baptist Convention of Malawi, MTh, University of Natal, 2003.

[86] Int. Marilyn Upton, Area 36 Baptist Church, Lilongwe 5.1.2001. Elizabeth Njolomole worked with Carolyn Swafford in producing this booklet in the early 1970s when Elizabeth Njolomole was national chairperson of *Umodzi*.

[87] See also Rachel Nyagondwe Fiedler, "The Place of Religion in the Struggle for the Rights of Girl Children: A Case Study of Experiences of Girl Children in Initiation Programmes in Rural Communities of Southern Malawi", *Religion in Malawi* no. 10, pp. 37-41.

Positives in the church chinamwali

Church *chinamwali* is better because it is culturally relevant, and it gives identity to the girls as well. It is culturally relevant because it uses the methods of teaching of the traditional initiation, through drama, songs, dancing, figurative language, symbolism and procedures. This is significant to the initiates in that they do not feel that they are missing out by not being initiated through traditional initiation. To those as well as the society, this church *chinamwali* achieves the same purpose in the girls as the traditional initiation. The fact that traditionally recognized *alangizi* are recruited for this church *chinamwali*, assures the girls and the society that this church *chinamwali* is credible. It is also important that the church *chinamwali* has almost the same length as the traditional one.[88]

This cultural relevance means that those individuals such as the chiefs and *alangizi* as well as *angolozole* can also benefit financially as they would if they were involved in the *traditional chinamwali*.[89] This is because church *chinamwali* continues to pay dues to the chiefs, *angolozole*, *alangizi* and *azina* in just the same way as they would if the girls went to traditional (*bwalo*) initiation. This cultural relevance is liberating to both the girl initiates and their mothers. Church *chinamwali* is even more liberating in that it has found ways of eliminating elements in the traditional initiation that are oppressive to the girls. The most significant one is the removal of the hyena (*fisi*) tradition. This was oppressive because the girl was forced to have sex with a man she did not love and who would not be her husband, and nowadays it would also be a very good way of getting infected with HIV/AIDS. The other oppressive element left out in the church *chinamwali* concerns insulting songs. This *chinamwali* conspicuously lacked such songs.[90] This is liberating in that it is less embarrassing to the initiates. Further, apart from its cultural relevance, church *chinamwali* makes a serious moral demand that is compatible with the Christian faith. It discourages loose moral behaviour and encourages responsibility and good behaviour towards neighbours and the

---

[88] This is different from the booklet initiation that takes only an hour or so.
[89] See Molly Longwe, From *Chinamwali* to *Chilangizo*: the Christianization of Pre-Christian Chewa Initiation Rites in the Baptist Convention of Malawi, MTh, University of Natal, 2003.
[90] This is different from the songs in Patrick Makondesa, Christian Initiation Rites in Southern Malawi. In this collection some songs such as 4,5,6,9,10,11 on page 11 for example could be classified in this group.

society, which is characteristic of the Christian message. However, such moral demand could be well complimented with biblical teaching.[91]

However, some of the elements in this attempt at cultural relevance are oppressive to the girls. Some of the actions retained in this *chinamwali* from the traditional one such as moving on the buttocks, are oppressive. The retention of teaching that is culturally based yet false is also oppressive to the girls. A good example is the teaching on taboos relating to menstruation and submission in marriage. Such elements must be removed and adapted to the Christian teaching in order to liberate Baptist women and their daughters. Some of the teachings relating to ATR were liberative in that girls were exposed to the cultural beliefs in their context. However, their liberation should not be in the practice of them but in the knowledge of them.

Recommendations

The booklet *chinamwali* should be forgotten because it is useless. There should be a serious attempt to facilitate the construction of church *chinamwali* relevant to each people group in this region with prior proper consultation with the grassroots people.

In the church *chinamwali* to be formulated, the church should continue to use the same cultural expressions like drama, songs and figurative language among others. However, certain cultural elements that are oppressive must be removed or adapted in such a way that women are liberated. This can easily be done without loosing the cultural flavour while maintaining the integrity of the gospel. Even though the gospel must be conveyed through culture, cultural elements that tarnish the gospel must be sacrificed for the sake of the integrity of the gospel.

Though this church *chinamwali* involved initiation in five major areas of a woman, prepuberty, puberty, marriage, and motherhood, and being a grandmother, the church should streamline its focus. The initiation on being a grandmother (*kuweramira ana*) is not important. Firstly all the required instructions a woman needs are already dealt with in other initiation rites. Secondly, it is full of symbolism and riddles which most of the participants do not understand. An understanding of this initiation could have been possible if after the songs a commentary were given.

---

[91] In terms of teaching immorality this *chinamwali* differs from some of the teaching reflected in the songs collected by Patrick Makondesa.

Unfortunately, although the songs and actions were crude and lacked meaning, the *alangizi* did not comment on them to give clarity. As such the church should scrap this initiation. However, I recommend that the church should retain the prepuberty rite, the puberty rite and the initiation for women who are married. The prepuberty rite is important although it is not allowed in this church in the South South, there are certain lessons useful to the girls that can be taught properly at such tender age. Such lessons include the elongation of the *labia minora,* sexual dancing and moral discipline, which are more effectively mastered while girls are still tender. Lessons relating to sex also need to be taught to girls at the pre-puberty age as soon as the girl is conscious of what is happening in this area. This is crucial in this age when sex education is done freely over radio, newspapers and the like. As such by the time girls reach puberty, they will already have mastered wrong behaviours that are not in line with their Christian teaching. It is therefore urgent, in this era, to teach children sex education while they are still young.

There is a general complaint that prepuberty initiation is unnecessary because the girls are still very young, but this needs to be revisited seri-ously. If we are not teaching them, others are doing it. Again this may be the best time to teach them sex related issues while they are still in a cool state,[92] and not conscious of their sexual feelings.

I suggest skipping initiation for those preparing to get married as it is practiced in some churches such as Roman Catholics.[93] This is because very few girls in the Baptist Convention get married through a church wedding.[94] As such, it would be good to include the teaching on marriage in the puberty initiation rite where a slant to choosing a marriage partner should also be added. A more comprehensive initiation rite for married women should be done after marriage. This does not imply that marriage issues should be limited to those that have reached puberty and those in marriage.

An introduction to this theme should also be done during the prepu-berty initiation. This is in line with many educational syllabi where topics

---

[92] To be in a cool state means to be sexually inactive. For more details on cool and hot state see Breugel, *Chewa Traditional Religion*, pp. 202-203.

[93] See Orison Chaponda, The Christianized Yao Initiation Rite of Mangochi Dio-cese, MA Module 2, 1979, University of Malawi. p. 5.

[94] See Rachel Nyagondwe Banda, *Women of Bible and Culture*, pp. 172-176. Most women marry through *chinkhoswe* weddings.

such as sex education are introduced in lower classes even though they are developed further in the higher classes.

Seclusion of initiates in the church *chinamwali* should be maintained in order not to lose the mystery that goes with initiation, an important element in initiation that might contribute to maintaining the credibility of an initiation ceremony.[95] This seclusion should also mean that women only should be instructors.[96]

Although there is in existence this particular church *chinamwali* in the Baptist Convention, this has happened more by accident. However, it shows greatly the desires within the church to have a Christianized initiation for the girls. I therefore suggest finally that for a well developed church initiation, the church should conduct a thorough research into the traditional initiations prevalent in the areas they serve, people's perceptions and wishes and use these findings to come up with suitable church initiation ceremonies that are relevant to the areas they serve.

This means that an exercise of pointing out the disadvantages and advantages, including suggestions is just the beginning in the exercise of Christianizing initiation rites in the Baptist Church. There is need to construct a complete initiation rite in this area, which can be tested and evaluated over time.

The other challenge is to decide whether such church *chinamwali* should be in written form or not. I suggest that there should be some documentation for the church initiation ceremony, but that at the point of delivery, books and Bibles should minimally be used, as such might kill the enthusiasm and momentum that comes with such ceremonies. However, the instructors should study the materials thoroughly and deliver them orally from memory. Since not only one instructor is used, whenever one forgets, her friends can easily remind her.

In the construction of church *chinamwali*, two key written materials need to be produced. Firstly, there should be a written document of a complete church *chinamwali*. Secondly, there should be a separate

---

[95] Lack of seclusion in the Christianized initiation in Mangochi Diocese was a deterrent to parents who wanted to send their girls for initiation. See Orison Chaponda, The Christianized Yao Initiation Rite of Mangochi Catholic Diocese: Assessing an Experiment in Inculturation," MA Module 2, 1979, University of Malawi, p. 13.

[96] No male instructors such as priests in Mangochi Diocese should be included (p. 6).

booklet as a training manual for the instructors.[97] It was a wrong idea to include these two materials in one booklet when instituting the booklet *chinamwali* in the Baptist church.

Memorization is important and will not only be exercised here. Baptist women effectively memorize liturgies at funerals and even at their weekly meetings. In other churches, a whole booklet of prayers such as among Catholics, or the catechism in Presbyterian churches are memorized. In fact one may be barred from baptism if she has not memorized such booklets. If this is the case, I see a great chance that a complete church initiation ceremony including songs and drama can be memorized and delivered orally.[98]

There should be no anxiety of leaving out certain important expressions in songs and the like because this is normal in oral literature.[99] Neither should there be fear to rewrite songs. Such changes are inevitable, as context, audience and even those delivering it change. This is also well demonstrated if the songs from the mock chinamwali and those in the *chinamwali* text in the appendix are compared. Although they are the same songs, there are instances when such songs differ in wording and even structure tremendously, sometimes changing the theme, but in most cases retaining it. Since most of the cultures of Southern Malawi are quite interrelated, some elements that are seen to be useful could be incorporated from other initiation ceremonies.[100]

The exercise of developing a church *chinamwali* should therefore be strict on maintaining themes but not necessarily the exact wording and sequence of songs. Such things depend on the mood, the audience and the deliverer. The *alangizi* who participated in the mock chinamwali also said that in the church *chinamwali* obscene words in the traditional songs are substituted with *eeeh* to suit the Christian atmosphere.

---

[97] This was also done in Blantyre Synod. See Felix Chingota, "Sacraments and Sexuality", *Religion in Malawi*, no 8, 1998, p. 34.

[98] Molly Longwe has made one such proposal in the last chapter of her MTh, *Chinamwali to Chilangizo*: the Christianization of Pre-Christian Chewa Initiation Rites in the Baptist Convention of Malawi, University of Natal, 2003.

[99] B.M. Lusweti, *The Hyena and the Rock*, London: MacMillan 1984, pp. 2-7.

[100] An example for such an inclusion would be the song: *Ndinyanyale akamachinda azimva kuwawa* (I can get disappointed, he will feel pain when having sex) from Patrick Makondesa's collection, teaching that a good understanding between spouses is necessary for good sex. See Patrick Makondesa, "Initiation Rites in Southern Malawi".

With the above analysis I believe that if Baptist women adopt these recommendations, they will be able to develop a church *chinamwali* that will be credible and appealing to the grassroots women to send their girl children to it for instruction, because it will be culturally relevant and compatible with the Christian message. Then the church will be giving instruction to these girl children that will be liberating and adequate to prepare them for married life.

APPENDIX

Grassroots Chinamwali: What is it?

Documentation as observed by Rachel Nyagondwe Fiedler from 21.-23.9.2000

Through participation in research and practical ministry with the Baptist women in the South East region, I won their trust and they invited me to attend one of their church *chinamwali* programmes. To these church women, this *chinamwali* is different from the traditional *chinamwali*. It was held in a church building, and was organized by the church.

Girls dancing in style at a church *chinamwali* in the South East region

When I arrived on the 21.9.2000 in the morning, I was told that the pro-gramme would start that evening. I took lodging at the pastor's wife's home, which was about 100 metres away from the church building. The afternoon was filled with the excitement of the event in the neighbouring villages. Since the programme was to start that evening, I decided to walk about in the neighbourhood, to catch the general feeling towards the event from the grassroots people. By this time, I had known a few peoples' homes and this is where I went. I visited three homes around this village, always in the company of friends. All women belonged to the Baptist Church. The common greeting this day was, "How prepared are you for the afternoon event", and the bye-bye words were, "See you this evening" or "I cannot come to the programme, I like the *bwalo chinamwali* (the traditional one) and not the church *chinamwali*". As I visited those homes and walked back to my host, it was interesting to hear informal comments about church *chinamwali* from women (churched or unchurched).

The majority of women thought that church *chinamwali* lacked important details such as dancing while naked, which is fun. Some women, even though it was day time when I visited them, had the freedom to give me a glimpse of what it was like if I went to *bwalo chinamwali*. They usually sang a song while wriggling their waist, and the observers would laugh at such a gesture including myself. Since I had never seen either *bwalo chinamwali* or church *chinamwali*, I was really apprehensive about what I was in for. Some women sympathized with me for not being able to attend a *bwalo chinamwali* and went ahead inviting me to one. This I am still to see in the future, as there were none any more in that season.

A deacon of the church, whom I visited before the ceremony, thought that the prayer at the beginning of the church *chinamwali* is just a rubber stamp. The reality is that they do worldly things (*zakuthupi*) in the programme.[1]

After a couple of hours of visitation at around 4 pm, I decided to return to my host, still in company of my friends (BACOMA women). I was delighted with the feeling of this important occasion.[2] By this time the road to the church, which I took, was dominated by groups of women (a combination of older women and girls aged between 5 and 13 years). The women carried loads of firewood on their heads and small bundles of which I could not guess the contents. I wondered what the firewood was

---

[1] This deacon was male, the wife is one of the friends whom I travelled with in the neighbourhood.

[2] Every initiate pays a fee in relation to her age and the type of *chinamwali* – younger ones pay lower fees. In addition each initiate also pays K18.00 for *Kukalamba kwa Mfumu kuti tili ndi chinamwali*. (To inform the chief that we have an initiation).

for as well as those small bundles. The women were full of excitement and talking, but the small girls looked subdued.

Before we reached the house of my host, I stopped by a small grocery and bought drinks for the women who were in that area. Little did I know that this increased rapport with the women in the neighbourhood. I later discovered that one of the women I bought a soft drink for was a star in *chinamwali cha bwalo* in that area. She was inspired to come and be with me at the church *chinamwali.* By this time, through informal interactions in the neighbourhood, I had learnt about the importance of having enough coins for the occasion. I therefore made it a point to change enough money into coins. I had about K50 worth of coins. In a rural area, this was quite a good supply.

I arrived at my host's place around 5 pm. Around my host's house was a grass fence. In this fence, I saw women and girls seated, waiting for the commencement of the ceremony. In one corner of the fence I saw three women, one about the age of 40, the other about 50 and the last around 70. They were sleeping on a mat. I asked my friends about who these women were and why they were sleeping at that hour in the open, thinking that if they were sick, I could offer them some *Panado* because I had carried a supply of this, in the event of such circumstances. I was bewildered to hear that they were not sick but that they were the *alangizi* and because they were going to initiate girls throughout the night, they needed to sleep before the event.

It was then time for supper. There were several fires made (now I saw the use of the firewood bundles) and each group cooked its own meal. I was served supper in the house, separate from my friends but I insisted that I eat with them. They were amazed that a town girl would eat from the same plate with them. I assured them that although I lived in town, I had lived the larger part of my life in a rural area.

After supper, I was called by the pastor who was inside the house at his dinning table. With him were his wife and one of his distant relations, an aunt about 70 years of age. I was told that because I never attended *chinamwali*, the *alangizi* wanted me to pay some money to earn my entry. I later learnt that all the girls who came for this function also had to pay a few coins.

They told me that there were going to be four types of *chilangizo* and I needed to pay for each one of them if I was to attend them all. I was already prepared for this and I thought I would pay quite a lot, but was surprised to learn that I needed to pay only K50 per entry into each *china-mwali*. I gladly paid K250.00. The pastor's wife presented the money and also introduced me to the group. They gladly received the money and welcomed me to participate in the church *chinamwali*. The pastor explained to the *alangizi* that I was a very important person in his church (BACOMA) and so it would not be proper for them to involve me in dancing or anything I did not feel comfortable with, and that I would be writing in the process and that this was related to my job. They did not object to this and asked me to be free to do whatever I liked and ask questions where I did not understand. Then before the *alangizi* left the room, the pastor asked them "where is that water of ours?" (*Madzi athu aja ali kuti?*)" and indeed they had a cup of this water in their hands. The *alangizi* told him that his wife had already drunk the herbal mixture. The pastor told me that women were complaining that there were no drums for the ceremony and this would task them a lot to sing without the beating of drums.

The pastor and pastor's wife told the *alangizi* that they did not want the drums to be used at their church. They did not want the neighbourhood to think that *alowetsa chibwana mtchalitchi* (they have introduced childishness in the church) and that they were the same as in the *bwalo chinamwali* where such drums are used. The *alangizi* women accepted the pastor's position. The pastor then told them that they had his blessing to do the church *chinamwali* and that they could go ahead and start.

This was around 8 pm. By this time, there was already lots of singing at the church by the girls. This small meeting in the house was really taking up my time, little did I know that the singing would go on for three days, and I would probably even get tired of it. There was no need to rush, because these songs would be repeated now and then at certain times. When the *alangizi* left the room, I asked the pastor about the water he asked from the *alangizi*, which he drank. The pastor said that the water was to avoid "*kupwetekeka*", literally to be hurt "*ngati wina angachite zoononga kuti zisandichite kanthu*" (so that if someone does something destructive, they should not do anything to me.)

The pastor then told me that I should preach a short sermon before they started. He told the *alangizi* about this while we had our small meeting in the house.[3]

I was then escorted to the church by one of the women and the pastor's wife in the company of the three *alangizi*. The group represented a combination of church leadership and *chinamwali* leadership (church and tradition).

I did not preach. I just talked about Proverbs 16:20: "Whoever gives heed to instruction prospers!" I did not preach because I did not want to change the mood of the ceremony. I wanted them to conduct the ceremony without being critical. I decided to give only a short talk in case I would speak words that would change the mood or direction of the event. After this, I opened the ceremony with a prayer. The pastor was outside listening. After the prayer, he went back to his house to sleep. The pastor's wife handed over the group to the *alangizi*. The church building is rectangular in shape. ¾ of it is the main hall where the Sunday prayers take place. The other ¼ is a small room, which would be called a vestry in other churches, where those leading the service would meet before they enter the main hall for the Sunday service. There is an entrance door from the main hall into the small room and then the small room also has another entrance door from the outside into it.

All the leaders in my group (pastor's wife, deacon and myself together with the *alangizi*) were in the main hall. Then the leader of the *alangizi* took a mat and covered the entrance from the main hall to the small room. Then the *alangizi* asked other participants to go inside the small room (the room was too small for everyone, so some stood outside), but the girls between 5 to 13 years remained with one *mlangizi* in front of the line. The girls were dressed in either a wrap around their waist or a skirt. The chest was uncovered. The wraps or skirts were of different colours. The pastor's wife and the deacon took me into the small room together with the other participants. I sat near the entrance because inside this room there was a lot of smoke coming from a little fire made in the mid-

---

[3]   I was later told that this was never done at such ceremonies and the pastor was just doing it to please me, to make the *chinamwali* look more Christian. The informant said she was really surprised at the fact that I preached. Only a prayer is usually offered at the beginning.

dle of the room.[4] The two *alangizi* were sitting around this smoky fire, so I wanted to be near where ventilation was better.

Unamwali wa ana

As we sat in the small room, one of the *alangizi* in this room blew a whistle three times and went back into the main hall and stood behind the mat. She led this song, which was joined by all those in the small room that knew it.

(1a) Nyumba ya mako	The house of your mother
Uziti odi, ee, odi, ee.	You must say, eeh, odi, eeh.[5]
Kamwini wapompano.	The son-in-law of here.

Meaning: To teach children that sometimes they go into the house, they are challenging, they enter the house without knocking, they should say "excuse" before going into their [parents'] bedroom so that in case their parents were naked, they should be able to have time to dress up.

As this one stanza song was sung, the women clapped their hands artistically, producing the same rhythm. The two *alangizi* in front, and the nine girl initiates one by one entered the small room. Each one of them entered with hands folded.[6] The girls' heads were also slightly bent forward.[7]

Each initiate who came inside the small room sat with her legs stretched and parallel towards the burning medicinal wood, her hands still in the same position and resting on her thighs and her head still bowing. The song went on and on and the whistle as well was being blown artistically following the rhythm of the song.

---

[4] I was told by the *alangizi* that the fire was made from wood that produced smoke which would chase the evil spirits away which would be intended to hurt the initiates and the *alangizi* by evil people. One deacon told me a story where at one church *chinamwali*, one initiate died after the ceremony and that her death was believed to have been through such spirits. The practice of burning this medicinal wood is referred to as "*kutsekera chinamwali*" (close off the initiation ceremony). Indeed it is meant to close off evil powers from hurting the initiates.

[5] I thank Mrs Janet Kholowa very much for her help with the translation of this and all the other *chinamwali* songs.

[6] They hold their hands palms up on top of each other.

[7] In this position, the girls looked really subdued. I think it was a sign of submission to the instruction which they were about to receive.

When all the initiates had come in and taken their positions around this fire, one of the *alangizi* started another song still accompanied by a whistle, which went on as follows:

(1b.) Kamwini wapompano, (solo) The son-in-law of here, (solo)
Ee, ee, Eeh, eeh,
Kamwini wa pompano (response) The son-in-law of here. (response)

This song, without any comment on it, was followed by another one that went like this:

(2) Ngolengole, Chapalamira, Ngolengole (idiophone)
 Chapalamira [name]
Eeeeee. Eeeeeh.
Munena zatatawo. (*alangizi*) You say many things.
Munena zatatawo. (all respond) You say many things.

Meaning: To instruct children, it is at the beginning of giving instruction *zatatawo* - talking about great things, many things. Chapalamira – no meaning is given.

As the *mlangizi* gives *ulangizi* (instruction), the sponsors[8] (women who brought the initiates i.e. aunt, mum, sister or so) drop coins in the palms of the initiates. The *alangizi* collect the coins dropped in their palms and collect these donations, which are then put together in a pile. One of the *alangizi* keeps the money. She also counts it. If the sponsors are not putting in enough coins, the *mlangizi* who gives the instruction, pauses till more is given. After this song, the following was sung:

(3) Munene wang'ono. (solo) You say small. (solo)
Wang'ono wina mawa. (response) The other small tomorrow. (response)
Wina mubwere nawo m'mawa, Another one you bring it tomorrow,
eee. eeeh.

Meaning: This song means they are continuing the instruction. They should concentrate on the instruction.

And without a break, they switched one song to another as follows:

(4) Chokuba, ee, To steal, eeh,
Musiye pompano. (response) Leave it here.
Chotukwana, ee, (solo) To abuse, eeh

---

[8] Sponsors are at two levels. There are sponsors who pay for the initiation of the girl; these would be male or female. There are also sponsors who bring the girl to the initiation, all female. These are the sponsors referred to here.

Musiye pompano. (response)	Leave it here.
Chokana, ee, (solo)	To refuse, eeh,
Musiye pompano. (response)	Leave it here.
Chonyoza, ee, (solo)	To despise, eeh,
Musiye pompano. (response)	Leave it here.
Musiye pompano. (response)	Leave it here.

Meaning: Some children are liars, they sing this song to make them stop. Some are thieves, steal from the pot. Some insult parents even about secret things. They are trained to stop, so that when they go back home they should change.

Then:

(5) A Lucy mundipereke kwa Kawoza, kwa Kawoza, eee, A Lucy ndiperekeni kwa Kawonje, Ndikavinire mwana wanga akule.

Lucy take me to Kawoza, to Kawoza, eeeh, (solo) Lucy take me to Kawonje, That I should initiate [literally dance to] my child so that she should grow. (response)

Meaning: The child should go to the instructor to listen to the instruction.

Then:

(6) Phumbwa kudya kachere,

Ndiponye bwanji muvi?

The phumbwa bird is eating the kachere fruit, How do I throw my spear?

Meaning: A child should not throw a stone in the tree. The stone can hit elderly people. Should not climb trees because she can fall off from tree on elderly people, to respect elderly.

Then:

(7) Namaleule, (solo)
Namaleule, (response)
Munyumba ya mwa amayi (solo)
Bala mwana kuleza (response) 2x

Namaleule, [name]
Namaleule,
In the house of your mother
Bear a child to rear.

Meaning: A girl is so much used to her father's home and once she finds the father naked and the father sleeps with her and the girl bears a child resembling the father. (The ladies testified that there are such cases of incest and even in this case, the child does not sue, in fact the mother knows about it sometimes, it is even with her consent). So this is to make sure the girls are careful with their fathers.

Then

(8) Katcha zili mu Malomwe.

Katcha [ideophone] are with the Lomwe.

| Wajando, wazoto, | Those who have gone through *jando*, through *zoto.*[9] |
| Machende achepe. | The testicles should be small. |

Meaning: It talks about women's desires being different and varying between circumcised and uncircumcised men to engage in sexual relationships.

The above 8 songs were concerning *unamwali wa chiputu/ana.*

Litiwo

This initiation is targeted at women with first pregnancy to tell them what they should do when delivery time comes, sometimes a woman who already has a child goes through this initiation if she never has gone through it.

(9) Mwandiyendetsa chimbelenje,	You made me walk naked,
Chino, chino, chino.	Completely naked (ideophone).
Chakwamayi chino.	From my mother's naked
Mwandiyendetsa chimbelenje,	You made me walk naked,
Chino, chino, chakwamayi chino.	Completely naked, from my mother naked.

Meaning: The initiate moves without being dressed except a pant, she moves on her buttocks while sitting. The aim of letting her walk on buttocks without dressing or with pant only is to remove shyness because during delivery she will not have clothes on. (But in this church women put on a wrapper.)

Then

| (10) Atiwire, eee, Atiwire, eee, | Sew for me, eeeh, sew for me, eeeh, |
| Atiwire litiwo. | Sew for me *litiwo.* |

Meaning: This song is sung as she starts *kupota khonje* (to weave a sisal string). The initiate is sitting while folding the knee to her face.[10]

As the song was sung, with handclapping, the *mlangizi* took *mafuta asatsi* (castor oil traditionally extracted) and anointed a drop on the mid-

---

[9] Wajando – *Mdulidwe kwenikweni* (circumcision) Chidototo – *Mdulidwe wapang'ono* (minor circumcision). Wachilomwe – no circumcision at their initiation.

[10] *Kupota chiwondo* (to weave chiwondo*)* – In those days *chiwondo* was a tree whose bark they used to soak in water and then they would make her wear it around her *chiwuno* (waist) till delivery. At the time she is supposed to cut her pubic hair, the *alangizi* puts oil on the initiate's face. If the oil does not flow down straight, the woman is unfaithful.

dle of the tummy of the woman.[11] The oil is supposed to run vertically straight across her navel towards the vagina. If the oil does not move in a straight line, it means the woman was unfaithful.

By then it was around 11 pm, and the girls were led outside the small room, to retire to bed. It was now time for the second type of initiation ceremony -"unamwali wa litiwo".

Unamwali wa litiwo

In this ceremony, there was only one initiate. The mlangizi and some women brought this lady from the main hall through the same entrance that was covered with a mat, into the small room. I was still seated inside the small room, as she entered with her entourage.

Everyone was clapping hands with the same rhythm. The lady sat as the girls did in the earlier chinamwali, with hands in the same position and her head bowing forwards. Her legs also stretched to the same fire (they kept on adding pieces of wood to keep up the flame).

After the song, the mlangizi asked the congregation who would be az-ina for this initiate.[12] One lady volunteered and came near the initiate. She was then handed by the alangizi the materials she needed to per-form the ritual. The material was sisal, some seeds and a small piece of stone.[13]

Then this azina took the sisal, bent one of her legs to the head. The other leg firmly standing on the ground in between the legs of the initiate. As she did this, the women in the room sang this song:

| (11) Njamajo, (solo) | Njamajo, [name] |
| Ee, Ajanyama. (response) | Eeh, Ajanyama. [name] |

---

[11] In this case, the initiate was not pregnant, but had had a child. But in reality, this oil is anointed when the woman is full term pregnant.

[12] I understood azina in practice as one who had graduated from this initiation and had mastered it well and was confident enough to perform the dramatized ritual of this initiation. She therefore was not the sponsor, nor necessarily a relative to the initiate. Actually, for unknown reason, there was competition to get this position. As the woman who first volunteered showed some hesitation at certain points, she was threatened to be replaced by others who were more knowledgeable. Fortunately, she proved her expertise and performed the ritual to the end without being dismissed.

[13] Each of these items has a traditional name that only those who have gone through this initiation know. Knowledge of these names is a proof to others that the woman has gone through such an initiation ceremony. Sisal is called terankulumulo, the stone is sanundo. Seeds are nkhwanje. The stone and seeds are called mbeu (seeds).

This song went on and on, and there was clapping from the group. The *azina*, although standing on only one leg, was wriggling her waist as she performed the ritual. The *azina* took sisal and split this piece of sisal into sections ready to weave it into a single cord. This took about 30 minutes and the *azina* was in this same position while continuously wriggling her waist artistically. When she had finished making this about 1 metre long cord, she majestically handed the cord to the *alangizi*. There was clapping and ululation to signify that the *azina* was an able graduate of this initiation rite.

One *mlangizi* took the cord and tied a knot. Then she started the *ulangizi* chorus *kunkhani, kunkhani*[14] and explained to the group the meaning of the ritual. The *teramkumulo* is worn by a woman during pregnancy around her waist. It is to be worn at the time the woman recognizes that she is pregnant and it is to be left around her waist till delivery time. The sisal is to be a thermometer for the health of the baby she is carrying in her womb. If the *mbewu* gets rotten, then the baby will be *nthayo* (stillborn), but if the *mbewu* is not rotten, then the baby will be alive.

After this instruction, the *mlangizi* asks the initiate to sit on a mortar. The mortar is right side up, just in the same position as when pounding maize. The initiate sits with legs apart and back straight, the head still bowed, hands still in the same position. Then a song was sung which went as follows:

(12) Mbuziyi,   This goat,
Muli atonde, eee (solo)   You are a male goat, eeeh.
Muli atonde.   You are a male goat.

Meaning: The woman has just delivered and the man desires the wife for sex before the child grows up. The woman refuses but the man is trying to trouble her – so he is referred to as a male goat, the way it troubles the female goat. The song teaches the man (because at this the man also comes with the wife) to wait till the wife recovers from her delivery wounds.

(13) Ndakulungiza. 3x (solo)   I have given you advice.
Mbiya ya monjo.   A new good clay pot (which has been fetched from the fire).

This anointing ritual is known as *chipendo*.

---

[14] This phrase was used at the beginning of each verbal instruction and sung only by who gave the instruction.

Meaning: This song was sung after the *chipendo*, and the oil must flow into the right place. If it does not, the woman may die of *chivuwa*. (The women never have seen such cases but think it happens). *Chivuwa* can be avoided if the one who slept with her husband is not present during *chipendo*.

The anointing is in real life done in the presence of a few women and if one of the women present ever slept with the husband of this pregnant woman, the pregnant woman would collapse and the pregnancy would get lost.[15] If this happens, the woman is said to have suffered *chivuwa*.[16] After this anointing, the woman went back to her sitting position on the floor. At this time she was leaning her back to the wall. It was time for another instruction. Then a song went like this:

(14) Anyozeni lero.	Despise them today.
Anyozeni lero.	Despise them today.
Mayi osanyoza, iye alibe kanthu.	The woman who does not despise, she has nothing (nothing wrong with her)
Kanthu kali ndi iwe mmimbamu.[17]	Something is with you inside the stomach of yours.

Meaning: If you are pregnant don't disrespect your mum, dad, grandparents, they will help you one time, when you are sick.

After this song, another song was sung. As it was sung, the *alangizi* dramatized the words in the song.

(15) Kuwotcha,	To feel hot,
Akukanga.	She is failing.
Kutanda, unya manyi mwana.	Kutanda [name], you produce stool,
Mwana asanatuluke,	Before the child comes out,
Uyamba kusanza,	You start vomiting,
mwana asanatuluke	Before the child comes out.

Meaning: Before delivery, you feel hot at the vagina and anus, and before delivery you produce stool and then the child comes. The aim is to describe how a woman feels pains before delivery, it is to warn her before delivery.

---

[15] I have no reports confirming such an occurrence. It may be mythical to teach men to be faithful.

[16] *Chivuwa* is similar to *tsempho*, which also mostly afflicts the innocent party.

[17] The song is sung to teach these girls not to disrespect their mother, they should know that they will also have a child who will do the same to her as she did to her mother. (meaning given by a *mlangizi*).

When they sang *kuwotcha*, the *alangizi* demonstrated how the woman feels birth pains. When they sang *akukanga* they showed how the woman should push the child out. Here they lay on the ground with their back and bent their legs, knees upwards and putting the arms around the legs and demonstrating how she should push the baby out.

When they said *Kutanda unya manyi mwana asanatuluke,* they remained in the same position and the message was in the words. It was that the woman feels like going to the toilet before the child comes.

When they sang *uyamba kusanza mwana asanabwere* the meaning was clear in the words that the woman begins to vomit before the child comes out. They reinforced the idea by dramatizing how one vomits.

After this song, another song was sung, again the *alangizi* sang it while dramatizing the words in the song.

(16a) Chetetete	Nothing is done
Zuwali, zuwali kukalowa	This sun, this sun, to go and set
Zuwa ndi kutuluka.	The sun comes out.

Meaning: The aim is to show that when someone is due for delivery, the pains began maybe in the night, the other day, you have not delivered. It takes time, this is to warn her not to despair.

At these stanzas, the *alangizi* had had one hand up pointing from the setting of the sun to the rise of the sun.

(16b) Kuyang'anako	Looking there
Sanabwereko.	(the child) has not yet come.

The *alangizi* looked at each other and signaled with their hands, that there was no baby coming out of the vagina.

The song teaches women not to rush too quickly to the hospital just when they feel birth pains. It may not be the right time to go, and those waiting for the baby might wait for a long time.[18]

By this time, it was around 3 am; we left the room and went for our little sleep. When it was around 6 am on 22.9.2000 I was woken up by singing in the church. I had neither had breakfast, nor a bath. I just brushed my teeth quickly and rushed to check what was happening. It was the girls singing and dancing from last night, they just did part of their initiation ceremony and indeed were more privileged than us in that

---

[18] It is culturally felt that if a woman delivers shortly after arriving at the hospital, she is competent and well schooled in this initiation.

they had slept from around 11 pm to 6 am. They were full of vigour and ready to start the rest of their initiation. However, the official programme had not started yet. They were singing and dancing outside the church informally although they made one circle only.

It was time for the girls who had gone through the *chinamwali cha ana* to show these new initiates how to wriggle their waist during sexual relations with men.

The new initiates sat inside the circle and the graduates from this initiation were standing around them. Most of them had a small cloth tied around the waist on top of their wrappers or skirts. This was to show the twists they made as they wriggled their waist. The graduates, a pair at a time, went inside the circle, while a song was sung, and they performed the sexual dance. They would then pick on any two of the new initiates to come inside the circle to dance in the same way, while they went to the outside circle. I saw that some of the new initiates danced even more skillfully than some of the graduates. It was fun.

Since it was daytime, writing was much easier, and although I was really tired by then, I was determined to record as many of these girls' songs as possible. The following were songs recorded on day 2 on 22.9.2000.[19]

(17) A Linly,	Linly
Perekani mtondo wotukwanira.	Send (back) the abusive mortar
Pereka, Linly,	Send (back), Linly
Pereka mtondo wotukwanira.[20]	Send (back) the abusive mortar.

Meaning: If you borrow a mortar from someone bring it back in time before the owner asks for it and is angry with you (there is a danger to not interpret words literary, but in certain cases, the words in the song have a literal meaning e.g. *mtondo* in this song is not referring to the vagina although in other songs it may mean such.

(18) Mayo, mayo	Sorrow, sorrow (ideophone)
Ndodo ya mfumu ndisaitaye.	The chief's stick I should not lose it.
Vala ingagwe.[21]	Wear it, it can fall.

---

[19] Although these songs were sung before the initiation ceremony started, all of them were sung during the initiation ceremony at different stages.
[20] One of the women sitting beside me said the song talks about a husband who marries a woman who is good at castigating people and the husband would proudly call upon her to shout at those who offend him.

Meaning: There is no meaning for this song, just like some songs do not have a meaning.

(19) Bongololo waduka mutu;   The millipede has lost its head;
Nati akalume.[22]   He wanted to go and bite.

Meaning: They have not been told what it means.

(20) Kadamanja, Kadamanja   Kadamanja (name), Kadamanja
De, de, de,[23]   De, de, de,
Kulaula amayi wake.   Defiles her mother (by dancing in a way that should not be mentioned publicly).

Meaning: This song is sung so that girls should not insult parents.

(21) Inu amayi, lero,   You mother, today,
Ndi amuna anu, lero,   With your husband, today,
Mwandiyesa chikwakwa[24]   You have taken me as a slasher
Chometera.   For shaving.

Meaning: Do not abuse children, some things can be done by you. The husband sends her this and then you also send her something at the same time this is not good.

(22) Matimati akuno sadyibwa.   The tomatoes from here are not edible.

Nyerere,   Ants,
Kaya ndiyambe ine   Maybe I start
Ndithamange misala, eee. 2x   To go mad, eeeh. 2x

Meaning: To tell the girl who does not fear to sleep with either boys or men. She has gotten pregnant and she is told that the pregnancy is the result of what she was doing. She was not playing.

---

[21] Not sure of the meaning although literal translation implies one is crying and then, the words in the second and third line say the chief's staff, don't loose it, put it on, it can fall down.

[22] Though I did not understand the meaning the song was interesting in the way it was dramatized by the new initiates. The initiates lay on the ground two by two, head to head, and holding each others' hands straight horizontally and rolling in this position many times like a millipede in the mud. By the end of this song the girls were a painful sight to look at, mud all over their bodies and heads. During this day, initiates did not refuse to perform whatever was asked of them, after all this entire dramatization was started by graduates of the initiation.

[23] As the song was sung, *de, de* was artistically demonstrated by twisting the waist in the sides rhythmically, suggestive of sexual relations with a man.

[24] Scott-Hetherwick: A large knife for cutting grass and reeds, or a short knife like a butcher's knife, or a sickle.

(23) We, we, we, Namawewewe	We, we, we, Namawewewe [a girl's name]
Ndinapita kwa bwenzi langa.	I went to my boyfriend.
Wewewewewe	Wewewewewe
Bwenzi langa anandifunsa	My boyfriend asked me
Namawewewewe.	Namawewewewe.
Zonsezi ndi zako?	Are all these (things) yours?
Namawewewe.[25]	Namawewewe.

Meaning: She went to her boyfriend and he asked her, are you not lame. These labia are all long ones? I am not lame, they are all mine.[26]

"Are all these things yours". This question is referring to the labia minora that she lengthened when she was still young.

(24) Izi zawona izi.	These have seen these.
Zawona ine.	They have seen me.
Kwathu ku Mulanjeko,	At home in Mulanje.
Amayi akayimba manja.	(My) mother was clapping hands.
Ababa akayimba ng'oma.	(My) father was beating the drum.

Meaning: Your dad and mum had to have sex and had you as a child. This is the way a child is born.

(25) Chiyang'anire chilikumwendo	Watch what is under/at your foot
Ngati amayi anachiwona.	If mother saw it.

Meaning: Means menstruation, you ask someone to check you if the mother also sees this, you should look after yourself when you are menstruating.

(26) Hinawone	I have never seen
Mbolo nayigwa.	The penis falling.
Amenewo simalaulo.	These are bad luck.
Amayi anati	Mother said
Mwana wanga kathune.	My child pull.
Ine natokana.	I refused.
Lero sizi	Today these are the things
Zandigwera izi.	These have fallen on me.
Ndikatokana.	I was refusing
Kapale moto,	Go and get fire,
Nalembeka.[27]	Nalembeka [name].

---

[25] The girls sang this song proudly wriggling their waists.
[26] This is one of the examples where the meaning given during the mock *chinamwali* obviously refers to the same song, but differs in interpretation.
[27] While singing this song, the girls danced with a fake penis made of cloth, positioning it to their vagina.

Meaning: It means the man is not sweet, it is a disease, if parents say No, don't do it because you can catch AIDS.

(27) Munyumba mwa amayi	In your mother's house
Mukhale mulitsitsa,	Sit decently (with your legs stretch out horizontally on the ground),
Munyumba mwa amuna anu	In your husband's house
Mukhale mulivekete.[28]	Sit anyhow.

Meaning: If you sit with your father, mother or anyone, sit properly and respect them, but if it is your husband, sit the way you like. Even if he sees your vagina it does not matter.

(28) Likita iwe,	You Likita,
Anzathu olemera,	Our friends who are rich,
Muvala nsalu zambiri.[29]	You wear many clothes.

Meaning: The rich one will put on twenty clothes but the one who is poor has only one. Do not ask your husband to buy you more clothes just because you have seen your friend's husband has bought her many clothes. Your husband should decide for himself to buy you what you need.

(29) Mkoko wa nthochi	A bunch of bananas
Siuchedwa kulemera,[30]	Does not take long to be heavy,
Mwanangulu.	Mwanangulu [name].

Then another song:

(30) Ee, ee, ee,	Eeh, eeh, eeh,
Chikuni chakolera,	The firewood has caught fire,
Ee, ee, ee.	Eeh, eeh, eeh.
Mwanangulu, unena ine, 2x	Mwanangulu [name], you talk about me,
Mwanangulu, unena aja.	Mwanangulu, you talk about those.
Chikuni chakolera.	The firewood has caught fire.

---

[28] As this song was sung, the initiates demonstrated how they would sit. The interesting time was when they demonstrated how they would sit in their husband's house. They threw their legs in the air, apart, showing their nakedness.

[29] The song was artistically demonstrating how a rich girl takes time to undress herself before going to bed. The graduates dancing this song deliberately put on as many pieces of underwear as they could, and as they sang, they removed the top dress first and then what they put inside the dress one piece at a time, like a petticoat, or a bra. (I was scared, I thought they were going to remove the pant as well, but fortunately I was saved from seeing the birthday suit.) But even with a pant alone, they danced for some time in front of their friends, unashamed.

[30] One of the women told me that the song means that if a girl is married to a boy who did not undergo initiation, he would weigh her down during sex.

Then another song

(31) Akachitole. 2x	She should go and pick it.
Chitole.	Pick it.
Akachitole ndi nkhongo.	She should pick it with the back of the head.
Akachitole 2x	She should pick it.
Akachisiye ndi nkhongo.[31]	She should leave it with the back of the head.

Meaning: A man desires to sleep with the wife, *chikuni chakolera* (the man is ready, has an erection) and he wants to have sex with the wife, and the wife's vagina also has fire and he uses his penis to extinguish the fire in her vagina.

(32) Anyundo kubedi kuja,	Anyundo [woman's name], on that bed of yours,
Anyundo ndi amuna anu,	Anyundo with your husband,
Mumatotani ku kada?	What do you do when it is dark?
Ndimangotere.[32]	I just do like this.

Meaning: To teach the children that a man does not have oral sex, but that sex is in the vagina.

(33) Tete, abale, sindinaone	Tete (name), friends, I have never seen
Khoswe naliterela mwendo	A rat slipping with the leg
uli khoma	into the wall (and)
Wina uli kubedi.	the other one is on the bed.
Abale ndikokeleni kukhonde.[33]	Friends, pull me to the verandah.

Meaning: It tells them when to do sex, we do like this, we do it upside down, sideways, backside.

(34) Jejemera, ee, ee, jejemera	Shiver, eeh, eeh, shiver
Mutu wako umagwera, umagwera	Your head falls, it falls
Bere lako ilo pilo	Your breast is a pillow
Mimba yako ndi matilesi	Your stomach is a mattress
Chiuno chako chimagwedera	Your waist wriggles
Chinena tikatole.[34]	Your vagina, take it (penis) in.

---

[31] The girl lies horizontally on her back and twists her head backwards till she picks a piece of wood under her head with her mouth. Then she again twists her head to put back the log under her head.
[32] The girls danced while demonstrating how they would engage in sex with their husbands in a standing position, two by two.
[33] The song talks about the position of a woman when making love.

Meaning: Your head shakes, your breasts, your husbands holds them, your tummy is your husband's bed, your waist is for dancing and your vagina is for receiving the penis.

(35) Dedeleka, dedeleka	Come out quickly, come out quickly,
Namwali tuluka nyumba	Young woman, come out of the house,
Thangate maliro	Help me with a funeral.
Mwana kulira wayamba kale.	The child started crying long time ago.

(36) Sinoya lero	Sinoya (name) today
Ee, Kalilombe.	Eeh, Kalilombe (name),
Ndamva kuti amayi amwalira	I heard that mother passed away at
Chipatala cha gulupu.	Queen Elizabeth Hospital in Blantyre.

Meaning: For some, if it is their mother who is sick, they don't bother but if it is the husband, they forget that it is their mum who bore them. It is also sung for *litiwo*.

(37) Sala, naona,	Sarah, I have seen,
Sala nawona	Sarah, I have seen.
Mwana mbalame,	The child of a bird,
Tiye, tiye kumanda.	Lets go, lets go to the graveyard.
Kwaitana, ee, Matebule,	It has called, eeh, Matebule [name],
Sala, nawona.[35]	Sarah, I have seen.

Meaning: If you try to discipline your child and does not take heed of the instruction, she will be in trouble, after you die she will regret because you will not be there to advise her.

(38) Gagadila, gagadila,	Have sex, have sex,
Chisoni amuna.	Sorry (my) husband.
Mwana natodwala,	The child is sick,
Iye nanditana: bwera,	And he calls me: come,
Tigagadile ga.[36]	Let us have sex.

---

[34] The song talks about how a woman responds to a man when making love. It also talks about the position she takes in lovemaking.
[35] Not sure of the literal meaning.
[36] The teaching is that the husband is not sensitive when it comes to sex with his wife, even when the child is sick, he calls for her to have sex with him.

Meaning: If the child is sick, the husband should not ask the wife to remove pubic hair, it is not time to have sex. The wife refuses but the man wants her. It is to teach men to wait till the child gets well. There are other diseases, which get worse with sexual activity, e.g. measles.

This singing continued but I was hungry, and since the official initiation for the girls had not started, I rushed to my hosts' house to have a quick breakfast. The *alangizi* waited for me, because by this time they had learnt that it was very important for me to observe as much as I could. They got used to my writing and asking of questions as well.

Chinamwali cha ana (resumed)

Around 9 am, the official *chinamwali cha ana* recommenced. Two rows of girls lined up with soles facing each other while sitting with their legs horizontally straight on the ground, along the church building wall One *mlangizi* was holding a live black chicken. It was time to start a ritual called *Chikwatu;* the first song was sung and it went:

(39) Chikwatu, gwira nkhuku.   Chikwatu[37] [a bird], catch a chicken.

Meaning: Children should not catch a chicken and play with it while the parents are there. There are some children who catch a chicken and insult it in the presence of elderly people.

As this chorus was sung, the *mlangizi* passed on a chicken to the initiates. When they got the chicken, another song was sung, while the initiates were still in the same position. That went like this:

(40) Nkhuku   Chicken
Nkhanga ndi ana.   Guinea fowl and chicks.

Meaning: It is time for the initiates to listen to the instructions. They should be quiet and listen. *Nkhanga* is the *mlangizi* and *ana* are the initiates.

The girls, as the song was sung, moved in a line towards the other side of the line while seated with their bottoms. They did the same and moved towards the other side of the line with their bottoms. This went on and on till the chorus stopped. Then the *mlangizi* started another song:

(41) Ndakudzula. (4x)   I have removed the feathers.
Tambala wa nkhongo.   The cock of the back of the head.
Namwali wavina chinthenga. (2x)   The initiate danced with the feathers.

---

[37] *Mthantauzira Mawu: Chikwatu: mtchitidwe wolanda kanthu mdzanja la wina.*

Meaning: The wife removes pubic hair of her husband. "The removed hair of the husband" this is to let them know that when they get married she should remove her husband's pubic hair. The husband can also remove the pubic hair of the wife.

The song comes soon after the girl has a feather on her head and dances the head only with the feather as this song is being sung.

(42) Kudzukudzu maweya, eee,   Remove the (pubic) hair, eeeh,
Kudzukudzu maweya, eee.   Remove the (pubic) hair, eeeh.

Meaning: It is similar to the one above; but it is also different in that it teaches girls to shave their own pubic hair because their pubic hair should not cut the husband's penis.

As the song was being sung, she was swinging the chicken in the air till the song finished. The initiates had returned to their sitting position with legs stretched out horizontally and their hands in the same position slightly in front with heads bowing low. Then another song went like this:

(43) Ndiuzeni,   Tell me,
Ndiuzeni nyini ya nkhuku,   Tell me the vagina of the hen,
Ee, eya, eya, eya, eee.   Eeh, eyah, eyah, eyah, eeeh.

Meaning: To tell the initiates that it is not only people who have a vagina, a chicken also has one. The chicken vagina is also used to teach the initiates "kuthona – kukoka" to lengthen the labia. Some girls refuse to lengthen their labia, because they say God created them well, why should they do it.

While this song was sung, the chicken was passed from one initiate to the other, and each initiate was asked to point at the vagina of the chicken. The *mlangizi* made sure that every initiate pointed at the right place till every initiate did it correctly. The *alangizi* had already plucked out some of the feathers of this hen from the vagina area to clearly show it to the initiates. As this ritual was taking place, the sponsors of the children were giving money to the *alangizi*. I also threw some of my coins just to enjoy the mood of the occasion although I was not sure as to the relevance of this activity to the Christian education of the girls. After this, the *mlangizi* started her song.

(44) Elele, elele, elele.   Elele, elele, elele.
Munena zatatawo.   You say many things.
Mungonena pang'ono,   Say just a little,
Wina mubwere nawo mawa.   Another one you come with it tomorrow.

Then she told the initiates of a mythical story that went like this:

The cock had sexual intercourse with a bird. It got a razor blade and gave it to the bird but the bird dropped it. The cock wanted his razor blade and told the bird that if she does not find it, he will die.

And then the *ulangizi* song above was sung again at the end of this story. The meaning of the story was not given at the actual *chinamwali*, but during the mock *chinamwali*.

Because the chicken lost a razor blade for *nakachibaye* (the hawk). *Nakachibaye* catches the chicks of the chicken, and the chicken up to now is searching for this razor blade in the ground so as to protect its children from being eaten by *nakachibaye*. Therefore when you borrow something from someone, make sure you take it back to the owner.

After this, the initiates were put in a circle and the *alangizi* took lots of maize husks (*madea*) and mixed it which maize flour and the initiates were asked to kneel around this wet mixture on the ground. They were told to beat the mixture with their hands. They did this continually as a short chorus was being sung that went on like this:

(45) Ozinyera,   One who has soiled himself,
Ozinyera.   One who has soiled himself.

Meaning: The initiates, in patting the *deya*, it is to subdue them, some are proud. Some cook *nsima* with *deya* and they tell their brothers to take *deya* (*nsima ya deya*). Do not mention *deya* because it is to insult their brothers because *deya* means that they are not circumcised. *Litsiro-deya* (the foreskin keeps *deya*). Again it is to teach children to care for the elderly when they have messed themselves up.

As the girls continued to pat this mixture, the mixture splashed all over their bodies, the face and their front was the most messed up with this mixture. I felt pity for them. And then after a while when the girls really looked tired after this exercise, the *mlangizi* started the phrase *kunkhani, kunkhani*, for giving instruction. This is what she said:

The *madeya* is not for you, it is for the boys. The boys who have not been circumcised are referred to as with *deya*. (The foreskin is *deya*). This is what the boys are told at their initiation camp. For this reason, when you get back home, don't speak to boys about *deya*, because it is rude to the boys. Also that if an old person has messed herself up, she should help to clean her.

As the *mlangizi* gave out this instruction, sponsors of the girls and well-wishers like myself threw coins at the plate of the *alangizi*. By this time I had realized that some were throwing maize seeds instead of coins. I asked one of the elderly women as to why maize seeds were used. I was told that these women had paid money in advance to the *alangizi* for this purpose and the maize seeds are just a sign that they have done that. I had already given money, and I did not have to continue to throw coins at the *alangizi*. I however decided to give some coins to some women to use it for this purpose. I saw some securing the coins firmly in their *chitenje*, and could not see them using the money for that purpose.

It was now around 11 am and we left the church grounds and were led to a nearby hut. The initiates were told that they were going to look for rats, and they were asked to pick good sticks for this purpose. All the nine girls got their sticks and headed for the hut to look for rats. This ritual is traditionally known as *"kusaka makoswe"*. Near this mud thatched house was a big tree. It was very hot, and I was happy to have this shade. By this time there were roughly about 200 women in total who had come to watch the occasion. The initiates with their *angolozole* went close to the hut together with the *alangizi*. I wanted to be in the shade under the tree but at the same time did not want to miss the fun at the hut. I decided to follow the initiates to the hut. The initiates were lined up in front of the hut in such a way that their sticks would reach the roof. The *alangizi* started singing this song:

(46) Saka, saka makoswe.   Catch, catch mice.

Meaning: They teach the children not to look at their dad when he is on the roof, because sometimes the dad may be wearing a torn pant and as such his private parts may show, it is not good for a girl to see him in this state.

At the song went, the initiates were told to continuously beat the roof of the hut to find rats that were in the roof.[38] As they beat the roof in anticipation to find rats, one of the *mlangizi* shouts *"uyu khoswe"* ("there is a rat") but is only lying. There is no rat. Then after a while the *mlangizi* sang the phrase *Kunkhani, kunkhani* and she narrated the lesson to the initiates. The initiates were told to put the sticks down and position their hands in the same way. She said this:

The hitting on the roof is demanded by your parents. They want you to know that you should not go under the house when your dad is on top of the roof. Your dad may have a torn pant and the penis may show and it is not good for

---

[38] This was a very dangerous exercise. The grass roof was very dry, and each time the sticks beat this roof, there were chaffs jumping onto the girls' heads and faces. By the time they finished the exercise, they were covered with this grass chaff. And together with the *madeya* mixture in the earlier stage, the girls were not happy.

you to see. But try to avoid this by maybe going somewhere till your mum is outside the house.

As this instruction was given, the sponsors and well-wishers dropped coins in the girls' palms. Then it was time to proceed to the bush, they were told other instructions concerning how they should behave when they go back home.

"Do not say *mbolo youma* (dry penis), *machende* (testicles)." They were told that penis and testicles are always covered with clothes *(zimakhala mu nsalu)*. *"Chinyini ndi cha nsalu"*, the vagina is also covered in the clothes and so do not scold people with such names. Do not agree to have sex with other men outside marriage. Be patient because there is a man reserved for you. Do not agree *"kulawa"* ("to taste") sex. If they want marriage, they should find you at home. You have nice breasts and your husband is going to play with them gladly.

Instructions in the bush

After these instructions we went out of this place and headed towards the bush. On the way to the bush we had a few stops, which I will refer to by numbers.

Stage 1, the girls were just showing off, there was no *mlangizi* but they made a circle and there was again lots of dancing and singing. I was wondering why the *alangizi* were not there, but they were preparing for a demonstration that I was yet to see.

I again recorded some songs sung during this stage. Some of these were already recorded before. But a new one I recorded went as follows:

(47) Mayi, eede!   Mother, eede! (exclamation of sorrow)
Zinthu zanga zanyekulira.   My things are assisting in sex.

Meaning: When you sleep with a man, it is the vagina that helps the man as you swerve like a basket during winnowing *(kusefa)*.

Then the *alangizi* showed up and led the initiates beyond this point in the bush, the crowd was following, and the *alangizi* stopped at stage 2.

At this point, there was a body of a small girl wrapped up in a cloth from head to foot. And the *alangizi* were the closest to this body. I was far but the *alangizi* called for me to step inside the circle so that I would see and record the instruction. Then a song was started that went as follows:

(48) Mtsikana woyendayenda, ee!	The moving girl, eeh!
Mwana wafera panjira.	The child has died on the way.
Anafera panjira.	She died on the way.
Mwana wachigololo	The fornicious child
Anafera panjira.	Died on the road.

Meaning: The initiate is told that the little girl died because she was immoral and was never afraid of sleeping with the elder. The girl should abstain from sex till she gets married. They should stop being immoral and be disciplined. This will help to avoid AIDS and you leave your parents in poverty.

After this song, the *mlangizi* sang the instruction song: *kunkhani, kunkhani* and gave the following instruction about what we saw; (each time *kunkhani, kunkhani* is sang, the other women respond by clapping together).

> The girl that you see lying dead along this road has died because of promiscuity. She had sex with a man and because she was young she died and was dumped on the road.

At this juncture, the initiates had believed the story and were crying profusely. They were comforted by their *angolozole* although it was not easy. (If I had not been told earlier on by the deacon's wife I would have also believed the story and cried, but thanks to her I was saved from this embarrassment).

The theme of the instruction is to restrain the initiates from having casual sex before marriage. The name of this dead girl is "*anafera panjira*", literally meaning "she died along the road." But according to the name of the events, this is called *maliro a ang'ono* literally meaning the "the young dead." As the *mlangizi* was giving the instruction, some were throwing money on the dead body.

Then the *alangizi* led the initiates to the next stage. When the initiates and the group were completely out of sight from this stage, one of the women woke up the girl who had nicely pretended to be a dead person. (I personally could see her breathing but this was difficult to see for the young initiates because they were afraid even to look intently at the so-called dead body.)

The money that was given at this stage was all given to the young girl who was acting dead, but not without warning. She was sternly told never to reveal the fact that she had acted in this way. If she did, something was to happen to her.

Because the *alangizi* were preparing for the illustration at the next stage, we again had a bit of time in the bush waiting from them. Therefore, we stopped at stage 2, where there was more singing and dancing, all the dancing with wriggling the waist.

Again some of the songs were familiar, I had already recorded them, but the following were new:

(49) Mwana mnyamata usagone 2x	Young man, do not sleep 2x
Utogona?	Are you sleeping?
Ona dina.	See my vagina.
Tandileke. 2x	Leave me alone.
Ndamwa mowa.	I drank beer.

Meaning: He should not sleep, but see his wife's vagina and sleep with her. It teaches that sometimes it is a woman who desires the man, but sometimes the man is not interested. It teaches that a woman should not request a man for sex; the man should desire sex by himself.

As the song was sung the girls would laugh.

It was time to leave this place and we proceeded to stage 4. Just as we were approaching this stage, we saw two women dressed in sewn up dry leaves around their waist, but no other clothing. Their body was painted with white, black and brown round dots. The face too was painted in this way. To the young initiates, it was a scary sight. One woman had put on an umbrella and the other carried a short handled hoe on her shoulders. And *alangizi* from our group, as we moved towards these women (creatures, in the eyes of initiates), sang this song:

(50) Nguluwe, nguluwe	A (wild) pig, a (wild) pig
Bwerera koko.	Turn there.
Nguluwe, nguluwe	A (wild) pig, a (wild) pig
Bwerera koko.[39]	Turn there.
Misala, misala	Madness, madness
Ndinali nawo	I had it.
Ndinato usiya,	I left it.
Kuba, kuba, ndinali nako,	Stealing, stealing, I had it,
Ndinatokusiya,	I stopped,
Kumenya, kumenya.	To beat, to beat.

Meaning: The song is to scare the initiates against rudeness.

---

[39] Meaning: pig, go back to where you are coming from. In this case, in the initiation programme, these women are supposed to be perceived as pigs.

Looking at the initiates, they were very scared. Actually the *anasongole* had a tough time trying to pull them to move ahead with the crowd. And then as if this was not enough, indeed, the fierce creatures returned but then there was a dead woman's body ahead of us. Some of the women were there with the body including Mrs Banda and pretending to cry shouting the name of one of the mothers of the initiates as being dead. At this juncture every one who was a mother to the initiates was told to disappear from the group. But this was a fact only known to some of us and not to the initiates. Because of this, the initiates believed that the mother of one of them had died indeed. The initiates cried again in sorrow with the daughter who was cheated that it was her real mother, crying the loudest. We joined in the crying. Then, the *angolozole* comforted the initiates, and the women calmed down deliberately because they knew it was time for an instruction. Then, the *mlangizi* started the instruction song again; *kunkhani, kunkhani,* and told the initiates to respect their mothers, chastising them against bad actions mentioned in the above song, that they should not steal, beat each other up, should behave themselves.

Then after this, the *alangizi* grabbed sticks from the bush and went near the dead woman dramatizing that they were wizards and were fighting among themselves to get the flesh of the dead person to their home. As they did that, they were singing this song, the body was covered with two clothes, and as this song was being sung they were removing the top cloth, pretending that they were to share the dead body.

(51) Kasende (2x)	Go and peel (2x)
Kasende	Go and peel
Kasende, Mulima.[40]	Go and peel, Mulima.

Then they sang another song, about fighting to take the body home to themselves. This song went like this:

(52) Nimunyamuleni	Let me lift you up [?]
Ndi chonde.	With please [??] or: with fertile soil.
Walimbana nditukule.	She (he) has straggled.
Walimba viso.	She (he) has become strong.

---

[40] The meaning is that one who has energy is the one who is strong and can lift the corpse.

In the drama, the two *alangizi* fail to lift the body and the last *mlangizi* succeeds because her wizardry is much more powerful than that of her friends.

After this dramatization, the *alangizi* took some herbs, some small branches of trees and scattered them on top of the dead body from head to foot. And then they sang a long song in which these herbs and branches were mentioned. As these were mentioned, they were picked up and shown to the initiates. The song went like this:

(53) Ichi ndi chiyani?	What is this?
Mapira, eee.	Sorghum, eeeh.
Unapirira yani.	What "sorghumed" it?
Ichi ndi chiyani?	What is this?
Maudzu.	Grass.
Anauzula yani?	Who got "grassed"?
Ichi ndi chiyani?	What is this?
Nansongole.[41]	Nansongole (a thorny weed).
Anasongola yani?	Who got "thorned"?
Ichi ndi chiyani?	What is this?
Nakhache.[42]	Nakhache (a type of biting grass).
Anakhatchira yani?	Who got "bitten"?
Ichi ndi chiyani?	What is this?
Kapinga.	Kapinga (a creeping grass)
Unapingitsa yani?	Who got creeped?
Ichi ndi chiyani?	What is this?
Pandula.[43]	Pandula. (a big tree for medicine)
Unapandula yani?	Who got "treated"?
Ichi ndi chiyani?	What is this?
Senjere.[44]	Senjere. (a type of grass)
Unasenjera yani?	Whom did you "grass"?
Ichi ndi chiyani?	What is this?
Nthula.[45]	Nthula.
Unanthula yani?	Who got lengthened?

---

[41] *Nansongole* is a type of thorny weeds, when you step on them, they bite.

[42] *Nakhache*, a type of biting grass. It also bites if you pluck it with your hands.

[43] *Pandula* means a type of a big tree, a type of medicine tree.

[44] *Senjere* also known as Senjere in English, it is a type of grass.

[45] *Nthula*: a kind of fruity bush. Its fruits are not edible; they are a kind of medicine for lengthening the labia minora. The herb is charcoaled and crushed into a smooth powder and some salt is mixed into it and then the paste is rubbed onto the fingers that are used for lengthening the labia minora. The salty charcoal can be painful on the skin but salt seems to be used as a disinfectant.

Ichi ndi chiyani?	What is this?
Bonongwe.[46]	Bonongwe (a vegetable).
Ichi ndi chiyani?	What is this?
Khumbwi.[47]	Khumbwi.
Anakhumbwira yani?	Who got "treed"?
Ichi ndi chiyani?	What is this?
Nthochi.	Banana.
Yinanthochera yani?	Who got bananaed?
Ichi ndi chiyani?	What is this?
Nkhwani.[48]	Nkhwani.
Ukhale nkhwani.	It should be nkhwani.

Meaning: They mention different types of leaves such as leaves of banana, and leave it on top of the dead body, leaves of pumpkin, *nasongole* etc and put them on the body, and they sing the song that goes with it.

After the song, the *mlangizi* sang the instruction song *kunkhani, kunkhani*, and told the initiates that they should recognize those herbs, grasses, and trees. Some of them were for food, some were for medication. If they are told to get such and such a plant from the bush they should be able to get it.

After this song, the *alangizi*, partially uncovered the feet of the dead woman and started singing the following song:

(54) Ndiuzeni	Tell me
Njira ya kumanda.	The way to the graveyard.
Ndiuzeni.	Tell me.

Meaning: *Njira ya kumanda*, to tell the children that they should not leave a person who is very ill. She might die in their absence.

At the singing of this song, I saw each initiate being led by her *angolozole* towards the uncovered feet. The *angolozole* held the smallest finger of the initiate and with it pointed at a certain part under the foot. This action of pointing is referred to as *njira ya kumanda* (way to the grave). The initiates are told that when someone is alive, there are supposed to be lines but if dead the lines disappear. After every initiate had accomplished this successfully, a second song was sung:

(55) Kufa, mayi,	Death, mother,
Kufa, kunayamba kuti?	Death started where?

---

[46] *Bonongwe* - a vegetable, the leaves of sweet potato plants.
[47] *Khumbwi* – a kind of tree.
[48] Nkhwani – a vegetable, pumpkin leaves.

Kufa, kunayamba uku,   Death started here,
Uku mpaka uku.   Here, up to here.

Meaning: It is to tell the kids that death begins from the feet and the last is the head.
Death never starts from head to toe.

As the song was sung the *alangizi* showed this progression with their hands, pointing at the feet, the body and then the heart.

Then the *mlangizi* sang *kunkhani, kunkhani*; and told the initiates how they could recognize someone dying. She also told them that they should treat sickness seriously, because it is the beginning of death. In this, HIV/AIDS (*edzi*) was also mentioned as one of the diseases to be taken seriously. After this another song was sung:

(56) Kupempha kwa akulu   The elderly requesting
Ndiyang'ana ndi maso.   I see by their eyes.
Chewu, chewu.   Turn and look, turn and look.

Meaning: The elderly request things by looks, if you wait to give an elderly person something only after she requests you, she will die with hunger.

And then the *alangizi* sang; *kunkhani, kunkhani* and said that the initiates should not only help the elderly when they are asked by them. They should see the elderly and sometimes they will see that through their actions, they are asking help from them. For example, an elderly person carrying luggage, if they see her, they should help out. Then the last song at this juncture was sung. It went like this:

(57) Nthanangula.   Words.
Nthanangula za kamwa.   Words of the mouth.
Nthanangula.   Words.

Meaning: To teach the initiates that when they go and chat, not to spread bad rumours because they can put their parents in trouble.

At this song, the *alangizi* told the initiates and the group to go and that they should wait for them somewhere, because they needed to remain behind to bury the dead body. I remained with the *alangizi* who were supposed to be burying the dead. When the group was out of sight, the *alangizi* told the woman to wake up. She was really tired but she was praised for doing a very good job, in the drama.

As the instruction was given, money was being given and all this money was given to the woman who was pretending to be dead. The mothers of the initiates, were also secretly asked to give money for '*ku-*

wombola nguluwe' that is to thank the women who played the pigs earlier on at this same stage. This money was divided into two to give equal amounts to the women who played 'pigs'.

As the dead body was being buried, the crowd stopped at stage 5 and they were singing and dancing informally. It was around 4 pm. Then the *alangizi* led the group to stage 6. At this stage, there was another corpse wrapped nicely into a white cloth. The initiates were told to make a circle around the corpse and told to jump over the corpse one at a time in a circle. As the initiates jumped, continuously in a row, the following song was sung.

(58) Kalulu   Hare
Kulumpha njira.   To jump the path.

Meaning: This was an unmarried boy and was staying with his sister. The sister used to cook *nsima* and eat with her husband but not give any to the boy and then he used to beg from others but could not get anything and he died on the way. The boy does not have a penis to have sex with a girl. If you have such a boy with no penis to have sex do not abuse him in this way.

After a while, one *mlangizi* said: *kunkhani, kunkhani,* and told the initiates the following; This corpse is of a boy. He was impotent and so he could not get married. As such, he used to live with his sister but after some time the sister got married to a nice man. This boy still lived with her. But the sister was very cruel to him. She used to give food only to her husband but she would deny her brother food. This time, the sister overdid it and while her husband was away for a few days, she denied her brother food for all those days, and as a result the brother died.

When the husband came and found that the brother had died because of hunger, the husband divorced her. The husband told her that he could no longer take her as wife because if she killed her own blood by starving him, she would also do the same to him. So the girl lost both her marriage and her brother. She was very sad and cried.

The *alangizi* explained to the initiates that they should learn from that story that they should love others as they love themselves (here she referred to the Bible). She told them that we should know that some men are created by God in a way that they cannot marry, they are impotent, and these also must be respected in the society. She said "if a boy *alibe chochindira amupatse chochindira ndani*? (does not have anything to have sex with, who can give him anything to have sex with?")[49]

After this, the initiates were told to line up in a row and sit, legs apart, facing the same direction. The girls were told to move on their bottoms, a distance of about 10 metres to the last stage in the bush.[50] They did not only move on their bottoms, but periodically they would sit up and face each other, then move with their bottoms till they reached the stage. As this was done, the following song was sung:

(59) Kalambe,	Go and ask permission,
Kalambe kwa Mfumu.	Go and ask permission from the chief.

Meaning: If you want to initiate your children you need to ask the chief for permission, that is respecting him.

(60) Nankungwi ndipatse khasu	Adviser, give me a hoe.
Ndikakumbire mankhwala anga,	To dig my medicine,
eee, eee, ee.	eeeh, eeeh, eeh.

Meaning: If you are asked whether they dig *livala*, you should tell them yes. And if they ask you how you dig *livala*, you dig it with a stick. If they ask what *livala* is, tell them *ndi tsitsi la manda*.

When we reached the place, the *alangizi* had a *nsengwa*[51] covered in pink beads. The initiates in a circle facing each other knelt down. Then the following song was sung:

(61) Chipande cha amunanga	The (wooden) spoon of my husband
Chautsa ndeu,	Has caused a fight.
Chipandeeee.[52]	The (wooden) spoon.

After this, another song was sung and it went like this;

(62) Chingolopiyo,[53]	The Chingolopiyo (a bird)
Chingoti deya, deya,	says *deya, deya,*
Nandichindapo, napuma.	Have sex with me and rest.

---

[49] Here reference is not just to any penis but a potent one.
[50] Stage 7. And this is called *livala* or *tsitsi la manda*.
[51] Scott-Hetherwick: a small basket, round at the bottom, and somewhat shallow.
[52] The basket was referred to as "a plate of her husband".
[53] A similar song though with slightly different wording is in Patrick Makondesa, Christian Initiation Rites in Southern Malawi, MA Module 1, University of Malawi, 1999.

| Mbolo yosavinidwa kulemera. | The undanced (uncircumcised) penis is heavy. |

As this song was sung, the initiates in this kneeling position dug a hole in the centre with sticks. When a reasonable hole was dug, the *alangizi* took a long stick about two meters tall and firmly set it in the hole. They took flour that was in the small basket and put it around the stick. The *alangizi* took away the sticks from the initiates. Then another song was sung like this:

| (63) Hamunachiwone chigulumunya. | Haven't you seen a swollen big toe. |

As this song was sung, they were given the sticks again. They were still surrounding the hole and then they put the sticks in the middle of the big and its second toe. Then one of the *angolozole* who knew best to dance, was chosen by the group to dance for each initiate demonstrating her expertise in dancing. She went around taking the stick from the initiate's foot with her foot and dancing, then gave it back to the initiate in the same way. This was done for each initiate. Meanwhile, the observers were throwing coins in the circle. This dance is known as *kuolotsa unamwali*.[54] (To bring the initiation across.)

The group was really impressed at the way this *angolozole* danced. In fact the first girl danced only a little and was told to leave the circle because she was not competent enough. I felt very sorry for her, because it was a public humiliation. I later learnt that she did not have a mother, her mother died some time back. I thought as an orphan, she should have been treated sensitively. Then the second girl was invited into the circle and impressed the audience.

After this dance, the group dispersed. There was no explanation by the *alangizi* concerning what had happened at this stage. It was getting dark, but it was a women's day and women were not panicking to go home. After all some were to stay for the night again. Others who went, also went home just to catch up on a few things and were to come and join the group for yet another night adventure.

I was very exhausted by then. I went to my host's place. Since the other occasion was to start later, I begged my hosts that I take a short sleep and that they wake me up before the ceremony recommenced. I woke up and had supper and went back to the church where the cere-

---

[54] *Kuolotsa unamwali* literally means, to bring the initiation across.

mony was to continue. The ceremony had not started but as usual there was informal dancing and singing outside. There were also some fires here and there. The women still cooked in groups as it had been the case with the last supper.

Unamwali wa chabulika

It was time for another initiation – *chabulika* - for the girls who have reached puberty. As usual, the girls who had reached puberty, three of them, entered through the entrance from the main hall into the small room. They sat down and hands folded, rested on their thighs, with legs stretched to the herbal fire that was remade by then. Then they sang this song:

(64) Tsegulire, tsegulire!	Open for me, open for me!
Ndakana, ndakana.	I have refused, I have refused.
Apanja, apanja	Those outside, those outside
Mulibe mwambo.	Have no behaviour.
Anyumba, anyumba	Those in the house, those in the house,
Mulibe mwambo.	You do not have behaviour.

Then, one *mlangizi* sang *kunkhani, kunkhani*, and said: if a man sleeps outside, and comes very late, you should not refuse him entry into the house, do not leave him outside because an animal can kill and eat him. If this happens you will be sorry. So do not be jealous with your husband.
After this, the *alangizi* sang this song repeatedly.

(65) Kamuone, eee,	Go and see her, eeeh,
Kamuone namwali wa tsimba.	Go see the girl of the initiation hut.

As the song was sung the *alangizi* frequently and gently pricked the initiates' breasts. One initiate, who was the youngest, cried at this act. We could see the girls' breasts stiffening as the *alangizi* touched them.[55] This was done to test them if they were really mature. After this, the following song was sung:

(66) Nyanyuwe, ee,	Nyanyuwe (name), eeh,
Nyanyuwee,	Nyanyuweeh,
Sesele namwali, seseleseee	Sweep girl (initiate), sweep for me,
Eeya, ee.	Eeyah, eeh.

---

[55] I think this act was very sensual, it really aroused their sexual feelings.

As the song was sung, the *alangizi* had brooms in their hands and were sweeping the floor. Sometimes they acted like sweeping at people, and people were acting to be angry. Then the *mlangizi* sang; *kunkhani, kunkhani* and said that the initiates should be polite when sweeping. They should not sweep around when people are sitting in their home. This would be impolite. Then another song was sung that went like this:

(67) Machakala ndataye kuti?	Where do I throw the monthly period linen?
Taya khonde. (2x)	Throw it on the verandah.

Meaning: the monthly period linen, you should dry in your bedroom, they should not be seen by others, you should respect your parents, and you also need to take care of yourself.

As this song was sung, they dramatized what the initiates should not do. One *mlangizi* would take the dirty linen, put it on wrong places for example on the window, the verandah, and so on. In a certain scenario, the *mlangizi* plays the initiate going to do some business at a neighbours home and the initiate accidentally drops the linen there but when confronted she claims that it was not hers because she is embarrassed. When she is cornered, she admits that it is hers.

Then the *mlangizi* sang *kunkhani, kunkhani* and told the initiates to care for the menstruation period linen properly.[56] When it is washed, they should keep it out of sight of people. They should dry it on their body. This is demonstrated as follows: A woman ties a string around her waist. She washes the linen and squeezes water out and fixes it onto the string firmly on her side. She takes the dry clean one and makes padding for her menstruation. As she moves, during the day, the washed one dries and then she can replace it with the other one in the same way. After this another song:

(68) Kande, kande namwali, kalikandila.[57]	Scratch, scratch girl, scratch [ideophone].

Then another song was sung:

---

[56] In Africa, most women cannot afford commercial sanitary pads, they use worn out pieces of cloth such as from an old dress, blanket and so forth.
[57] I did not understand this song but the woman took the linen and washed it in a cooking pot. I guess it was to teach not to wash the sanitary materials in kitchen utensils.

| (69) Manika, Manika, Manika | Manika [name], Manika, Manika, |
| Anawa achiwona | These children will see it. |

Meaning: many girls during monthly period, some dry them outside on the verandah not inside, because it is obscene. If you let others see them, it means "walaula" (you have done something [culturally] offensive).

A *mlangizi* put on a period linen in the wrong way so that everyone could see it protrude. Meanwhile, the other *mlangizi* pointed at it and was disapproving the practice with gestures. Then the other *mlangizi* put on the linen in a way that it was not showing at the bottom. And she proudly walked around, showing to the initiates that, that was the way they should use the linen. Then another song was sung:

(70) Choyenda ndi ana	To go with children
Ndalapa lero.	I have stopped today.
Mwana machakala	The monthly period linen
Salala mbiyamu.	Put (?) in the big (clay) pot.

Meaning: The song teaches girls not to use the same washing pot with their mother when in monthly period. Doing this would prove that you have been to the *tsimba*.

As the song was sung, the two *alangizi* played the role of daughter and mother. They both were using one container to wash their monthly period linen. In the drama, the mother goes to one of her confidants and complains at her daughter's behaviour.[58] After this another song was sung,

(71) Achule, achule, ng'oma zangazo.[59]   Frog, frog, those my drums.

Meaning: There is a demonstration of a man who had slept with a woman in this state and one of his testicles has swollen up. The man cannot put on trousers but a wrapper because of the disease he has caught from the woman. Meaning is not in the song but in the drama.

Then another song was sung:

(72) Ndithu, ndithu,	Indeed, indeed,
Ndi amako ndithu,	She is indeed your mother,
Ngakhale ukhale ukula thupi.	Though you may be stout.
Ndi amako ndithu.	She is indeed your mother.[60]

---

[58]   The daughter should wash her linen in a separate container from her mother's.
[59]   I did not get the meaning when the song was performed.
[60]   See a similar Chichewa proverb: "Mako ndi mako usamwone kuchepa mwendo". See J.C. Chakanza, *Wisdom of the People: 2000 Chinyanja Proverbs and Figurative Sayings*, Blantyre: CLAIM-Kachere, 2001, proverb no 755.

Meaning: Many girls, when their mum is slimmer than they, they do not respect her but they forget that she is the one who bore them.

The song teaches the initiates to respect their mothers even if their physical form is inferior to theirs. After this, another song went like this:

(73) Chikwirire, chikwirire, chikwirire   Cover it, cover, it cover it,
Ukapanda kuchikwirira,   If you don't cover it,
Anawa achiwona.   These [uninitiated] children will see
                                           it.

This song was just to emphasize that they should not let the young children see their monthly period linen.

After this song, the three *alangizi* took mouthfuls of water and spit it all over the bodies of the initiates. The youngest initiates were very angry at this time judging from their facial expression.[61] After this they sang another song;

(74) Thong'ondo waza   Mouse has come, mouse.[62]
ndongonde.[63]

After this, there was another song:

(75) Nanchengwa, usamba mutu   Nanchengwa [a girl's name],
Usamba mutu   You wash your head,
Uleka uko.   (But) there you leave out.

Meaning: the song is about you, don't just wash the head, wash also the private parts to avoid bad smell. *Uko – kumpheto –* vagina.

As the word *uko* was mentioned, the *alangizi* pointed at the vagina area of the initiates. The initiates were advised to wash their vagina properly, not just their head. After this another song went:

(76) Mache Machado,   Mother of Machado,
Wandidyetsa dokola.   You gave me bad things to eat.
Mache Machado, ee,   Mother of Machado, eeh,
Wandidyetsa umve.   You gave me unhygienic food to
                                 eat.

---

[61] In my opinion this was very dehumanizing. They even spit the water into the girls' faces. I think, if there was a lesson to teach them, it could have been done without this.
[62] Translation not found. *Thong'ondo* is a type of mouse. *Waza* may mean to come or to sprinkle (*waza madzi*).
[63] I did not get the meaning or the purpose of the song.

| Wagwira magazi ugawa ndiwo, | You have touched blood and dished out relish, |
| Wandidyetsa dokola. | You gave me bad things to eat. |

Meaning: Do not cook and share food before washing your hands so that you do not contaminate your husband.

The song is aimed at teaching the girls to be clean when they are menstruating. They should wash hands after touching the linens so that they do not contaminate others. After this, the *alangizi* sang another chorus;

(77) Chinyela, chinyela	Chinyela, chinyela
chitha amuna	finishes (kills) the men
Akazi natsala.	Women remaining.

Meaning: If you have monthly period you see blood that is red, and when you finish the blood flow you see the black stuff (charcoal) and if you know that now you have finished your monthly period, you see white stuff and this is when you can now have sex with a man.

The women testified that there are people who have indeed suffered from *chinyela*.[64] These slept with a woman who had aborted. There is medicine for *chinyela* but the patient needs to report fast enough that he has slept with such a woman. Some of the symptoms include tummy upset, loss of hair and liking to stay in the sun just like someone suffering from AIDS.

As the song was sung, the *alangizi* showed the initiates the process through which the menstruation goes through using flour, curry powder and charcoal powder. Blood is represented by curry powder, flour represents the white stuff and charcoal represents the black stuff.

The *alangizi* put the powders in a heap together without mixing them up. Then one by one, the initiates were told to point at whatever powder was referred to according to their advice. For example they would say, which powder shows that you are ready for sexual intercourse, and the initiates pointed at the flour. Which powder shows that you cannot sleep with a man, they pointed at both the black and red stuff. Which stuff is the most dangerous and can kill a man? They point at the black stuff. Then the *mlangizi* sang *kunkhani, kunkhani*. And she said this:

Do not sleep with a man when you see the black stuff of the monthly period. It kills a man. Your husband must be told of the state in which you are by the use of beads. Display the white beads and smear the floor with fresh mud if

---

[64] In other areas *kanyela* is used instead.

you have finished menstruation. When your husband comes into the house and sees this, he will know that it is the time to resume sex. Similarly display black beads for black stuff and red beads for blood, as a warning to the husband.

After this instruction, the *azina* of the initiates bowed over the heaps of flour. The *alangizi* and the *azina* took the heap of the mixed flour outside. The initiates went with them. They went into the bush and in the presence of the initiates they dug a small hole and put the flower in there.

| (79) Watola mphande, | You have picked the *mphande*[65] |
| Watola mphande ndi manja. | You have picked the *mphande* with the hands. |

Meaning: The song signifies secrecy of where the first menstruation linen is hidden by the *alangizi*. As the song is sang they dramatize about their lack of knowledge about where they have hidden the linen cloth. They echo the drama by shouting "we have buried it in the pit". The linen is buried to avoid *chikawo*, something like *tsempho* that some can use it to harm others.

We could have continued to look at *chinamwali choweramira ana*, they unfortunately could not sing because they did not go through that kind of initiation.

Then they told the initiates to kneel around the hole and told them to bury the stuff but stumping their palms on the hole (there was lots of dust in the air at this time.). The initiates were very dusty by then. The *alangizi* took some mixture from the ground and gave it to each initiate and they were told to put it firmly in their palms and with their *azina* to go and have a bath. The *azina* should pour water all over their bodies while the girls hold the flour firmly, not allowing the flour to get wet. If the flour got wet, they would not be able to have children.

This was the end of *chinamwali cha chabulika*. It was now time for another *chinamwali* known as *kuweramira ana*, for mothers.

Kuweramira ana

There came three women initiates who were to go through this initiation. They sat inside the room, hands folded, legs stretched horizontally, towards the fire. The *alangizi* had a small basket and they took a sorghum branch out of the basket and put it on the ground. The women were to

---

[65] *Mthanthauzira Mawu a Chinyanja*: "Chinthu chomwe akazi amavala mkhosi ngati mkanda", something which women wear around the neck like a belt – The meaning may be somewhat literal.

beat out seeds from this branch with their bottoms. As this was done, this song was sung:

| (80) Akuwomba ndi matako | She beats with the buttocks |
| Mapira, eee. | Sorghum, eeeh. |

And then another one:

(81) Chimera cha mwana wanu,	The sprouted maize of your child,
Tibwerekeni mwana lichero.	Let us borrow the winnowing basket.
Ndanzanu ndato sumidwa,	Your friend, I am in need of something,
Lichero ndilibe. 2x	I have no winnowing basket.

As the songs went, the initiates crushed the millet with their bottoms and then tried to sift them with their palms. The *alangizi* collected all the millet that was crushed and put it on a white cloth. After this, another song was sung:

(82) Mpheta,	Mpheta [a bird],
Tola mapira,	Pick up the sorghum,
Tola mapira.	Pick up the sorghum.

As this song went, the initiates were told to collect the remaining millet grains, which were still on the ground. Each initiate collected the seeds and gave them to the *alangizi*. These seeds were put in a clay pot that was placed in the middle.

The *alangizi* saw that the people were not giving money as this was going on. They therefore decided to keep quiet and told the group that they were not going to continue until they saw that the giving was good. The crowd was angry at the *alangizi* because they thought enough money had been given to them and that they should not complain.

After a while, the *alangizi* continued as more money was given. And this song was sung:

(82)Wakolana ndindi,	They held each other very firmly,
wakolana.	they held each other,
Eee, yele, yele.	Eeeh, yele, yele.
Wakolana ndindi,	They held each other very firmly,
Wakolana.	they held each other.

As this song was sung, the *azina*, one for each initiate, also came and sat opposite the initiates. The *azina* lifted the legs of the initiate and placed them on theirs each resting on each side of her waist. Then as the song went, the *azina* moved with her bottom little by little towards the initiate, while dancing and lifting the legs of the initiates to the squatting position.

After this, another song was sung that went like this.

(83) Sunkhu, sunkhu, sunkhunya;   Shake, shake, shake!
Sunkhu, sunkhu, sunkhunya.   Shake, shake, shake!

The initiates sat back in their original position and then other women who had gone through the initiation came in one by one and danced to these initiates while this song was sung.

The women who danced, removed their clothes and remained with their pants: Each one of them had lots of beads around the waist. The beads were artistically connected to each other into a band of about 10 cm. In this attire they shook their bottoms but only from the waist to the knees. The other part of the body remained firm except the hands. The initiates were just watching the dance. This went on and on, and it was far too long for me.

Then there was a break and the following song was sung:

(84) Chiwali, chiwaliwali   Something   shining,   something
                               shining
Cha mwananga.   Of my child.

Then another one, which went like this:

(85) Namuyoyo,   Namuyoyo [name of an initiate],
eeee,   eeeeh,
Namuyoyo.[66]   Namuyoyo.

As they sang this song, they took the millet and put it on the hands of the initiates. And they sang another song:

(86) Limbe wathira,   Limbe [name] you have spilled,
Iya.   Iyah.
Limbe wathira,   Limbe, you have spilled,
Iya.   Iyah.

Then they sang another one:

(87) Chimera ichi   This sprouted millet
Mukagulitse.   Go and sell it.

---

[66] Meaning not clear to me, and it was not explained to the participants.

As the above song was sung, the *alangizi* danced. Another song was sung:

(88) Aliya, eeee,	Aliya [name], eeeeh,
Dzulo, Aliya	Yesterday, Aliya
Lero, Aliya	Today, Aliya
Aliya tikakumane	Aliya, let's go and meet
kwa Majawa.	at Majawa's place.

Then, the *alangizi* said these words:

Some use dust instead of millet and that in this initiation, the audience may have noticed that she has done things differently, it was because she believes as Christians we should refer to the Bible and Jesus.

Then she went on with other songs:

(89) Iya, iya, ee, ee,	Iyah, iyah, eeh, eeh,
Iya.	Iyah.
Njere, njere za mwana	The small seeds, the small seeds[67]
	of the child

As this song was sung, the *mlangizi* held a small basket with maize flour and continued the song:

(90) Njere, njere, njere.	The small seeds, the small seeds,
	the small seeds.

Then she sang another song

(91) Mazembeza	The habit of hiding something[68]
Mwaziwona.	You have seen them.

Then she sang another one that went on like this:

(92) Likoko, likoko,[69] ee,	Likoko, Likoko, eeh,
Likoko la mwana.	Likoko of the child.

After this, we moved onto another initiation. It was now around 2 am of 23.11.2000. By this time, I was very tired. But the women were not tired because certain women came only for a certain type of *chinamwali* and if that was over they went to rest. No one is allowed to see a type of *china-*

---

[67] Scott-Hetherwick: "*Njere*, the small seeds of tobacco, or of other flowers, vegetables, grasses, Indian hemp, terere, chitowe &c.".
[68] Scott-Hetherwick: "*zembeza*, to hide something, as a thief".
[69] This may be a rite.

mwali if she has not gone through it.[70] But for me, I got a ticket to participate in all and this wore me out. However I held on and observed the last initiation this night, that of *wachidzukulu*. There were three women going through this initiation.[71]

Wachidzukulu

Just like in the other initiation, the women sat, hands folded and heads bowing a little.

The *alangizi* asked the sponsors of the initiates to give the money needed. They had to pay K55 per person. I still remember one of the initiates crying because she was already inside the room but her sponsor would not release the money. The *alangizi* threatened that if she did not pay the contribution, she should not be part of the group. Then one of the church women begged the *alangizi* to take the initiate outside first for a chat. We were all waiting inside and then they came back inside. Apparently, this church woman was so touched and decided to lend the initiate the money. Then the initiation ceremony started.

The *alangizi* took sticks with flames and were dancing with the sticks swerving them front and back. The room was also dark, the lamps had no oil by this time. The *alangizi* had money but could not buy oil for the lamps. The audience was not in favour of their greed. I asked why the church did not buy oil for this occasion, I was told that it is normally the responsibility of the *alangizi*. and even though I had bought enough paraffin oil for the pastor, the pastor's wife refused that it be used for this purpose. I was not impressed. The women were now using just the grass to keep a small light going.

After the dancing with sticks, volunteers from the group came to demonstrate another dance, which involved sitting in a squatting position and then sliding both legs from side to side. This went on and on. I could not catch the purpose of the dance. I was tired and left to retire to bed around 3 am of 23.11.2000, leaving the ceremony in session.

On 23.11.2000, it was the end of the initiation. All the initiates were to come for a closing ceremony at around 11 am. My transport back to town arrived around 8 am. I was exhausted, had not had proper meals and could not wait to go back to town. So I left without being part of the clos-

---

[70] However there might be other reasons such as being hot or cool, or sexual activity, child birth or not.
[71] Their ages were about 40 years.

ing ceremony. However I bid farewell to the *alangizi* and thanked them for their support during the exercise and I also thanked my hosts and the women that had been my guides.

BIBLIOGRAPHY

Banda, Rachel Nyagondwe, *Women of Bible and Culture. Baptist Convention Women in Southern Malawi*, Zomba: Kachere, 2005

Breugel, J.W.M. van, *Chewa Traditional Religion*, Blantyre: CLAIM-Kachere, 2001.

Buku la Alangizi. Baptist Convention of Malawi, Lilongwe: Baptist Publications, nd.

Chakanza, J.C., "The Unfinished Agenda. Puberty Rites and the Response of the Roman Catholic Church in Southern Malawi, 1940-1994", *Religion in Malawi* no 5, 1995.

Chakanza, J.C., *Wisdom of the People: 2000 Chinyanja Proverbs and Figurative Sayings*, Blantyre: CLAIM-Kachere, 2001.

Chaponda, Orison, The Christianized Yao Initiation Rite of Mangochi Catholic Diocese: Assessing an Experiment in Inculturation, MA module 2, Department of Theology and Religious Studies, University of Malawi, 1997.

Chingota, Felix, "A Historical Account of the Attitude of Blantyre Synod of the CCAP towards Initiation Rites," in *Religion in Malawi*, no 5, 1995 pp. 8-15.

Chingota, Felix, "Sacraments and Sexuality", *Religion in Malawi*, no 8, 1998, pp. 34-40.

Fiedler, Klaus, "Christianity and African Culture, Conservative German Protestant Missionaries in Tanzania, 1900-1940", Blantyre: CLAIM-Kachere, 1999.

Fiedler, Klaus, "Bishop Lucas: Christianization of Traditional Rites, the Kikuyu Female Circumcision Controversy and the Cultural Approach of Conservative German Missionaries in Tanzania," in Robin Lamburn, *From a Missionary's Notebook. The Yao of Tunduru and other Essays*, Saarbrücken, 1991.

Ignasio, Elvira M, The Christianization of the Traditional Pre-Puberty and Puberty Rites for Girls and its effects on the Society around Nankhwali area, Monkey-Bay, BA, Department of Theology and Religious Studies, University of Malawi, 1998.

Longwe, Molly, From *Chinamwali* to *Chilangizo*: the Christianization of Pre-Christian Chewa Initiation Rites in the Baptist Convention of Malawi, MTh, University of Natal, 2003.

Makondesa, Patrick, Christian Initiation Rites in Southern Malawi, MA Module 1, Department of Theology and Religious Studies, University of Malawi, 1999.

Mgeni, Martin, Girls' initiation in a Yao Setting and Christian Attitude: Case Study at Msembuka Village – Chikala Plateau – TA Chamba, Msondo Rite. Class Presentation, Department of Theology and Religious Studies, University of Malawi, 1996.

Phiri, Isabel Apawo, *Women, Presbyterianism and Patriarchy. Religious Experience of Chewa Women in Central Malawi*, Blantyre: CLAIM-Kachere 1997, [2]2000.

Phiri, Makhaza Sylvester Saukani, Puberty Rites for Girls in Mlefu-Mbemba Village in Traditional Authority Mzukuzuku at Embangweni in South Mzimba, BEd, 2001.

Sakaike, Renata, Collection of Materials, Nsondo Rite, University of Malawi, 1996.